Complete Book of WINDOW TREATMENTS & CURTAINS

Traditional &
Innovative Ways
to Dress Up
Your Windows

CAROL PARKS

A Sterling/Lark Book
Sterling Publishing Co., Inc.   New York

Editor: Carol Taylor
Art Director: Dana Irwin
Photography: Evan Bracken
Illustrations: Kay Stafford
Production: Elaine Thompson, Dana Irwin

Library of Congress Cataloging-in-Publication Data
Parks, Carol
    Complete book of window treatments and curtains: traditional
and innovative ways to dress up your windows / Carol Parks.
        p.   cm.
    "A Sterling/Lark book."
    Includes index.
    ISBN 0-8069-0612-X
    1. Drapery.   2. Drapery in interior decoration.   I. Title.
TT390.P37   1994
747'.3–dc20   93-39113
                                                            CIP

10 9 8 7 6 5 4 3 2 1

A Sterling/Lark Book

Published in 1994 by Sterling Publishing Co., Inc.
387 Park Ave. S., New York, NY 10016

Created and produced by Altamont Press, Inc.
50 College St., Asheville, NC 28801

© 1994, Altamont Press

Distributed in Canada by Sterling Publishing,
c/o Canadian Manda Group, P.O. Box 920, Station U, Toronto,
    Ontario M8Z 5P9
Distributed in the United Kingdom by Cassell PLC, Villiers House,
    41/47 Strand, London WC2N 5JE, England
Distributed in Australia by Capricorn Link (Australia) Pty Ltd.
    P.O. Box 6651, Baulkham Hills, Business Centre, NSW 2153, Australia

ISBN 0-8069-0612-X

Complete Book of WINDOW TREATMENTS & CURTAINS

■ C O N T E N T S ■

INTRODUCTION

At some point in time the term "window treatment" replaced the more mundane "draperies" and "curtains" to describe the functional or decorative covering hung over the glass. A window *deserves* a special treatment! It is a very special element in the room, sometimes the room's single most important feature.

A window treatment is the application of creativity to plain curtains or draperies. A treatment can be anything done to a window to enhance it, cover it, emphasize it, play it down, hide it altogether, or just decorate it. A window treatment certainly can include curtains or draperies, but also may involve shades, swags, trim painting, decorative rods, faux finishing, replacing a pane with custom-designed leaded glass, painting a vine up the wall alongside, or perhaps simply leaving it bare.

In this book we have gathered the ideas of many talented professional designers. We hope the photographs of their work will give you an idea of the tremendous potential for creative window treatment design. We have provided you, too, with some expert guidance through the important steps in planning a design, and thorough instruction in the sewing and other techniques necessary to making your plan a reality.

Many professionals in the field have contributed their ideas and their expertise to this book—designers, drapery makers, installation specialists, and people who sell decorator fabrics and hardware. Their experiences and suggestions are meant to give you the benefit of professional help from the very beginning of your project.

Most of all, we hope this book will inspire you to develop your own unique window treatment designs, styles that reflect your own personality and suit your own needs. And we hope your finished projects will give you years of enjoyment.

PLANNING

YOUR WINDOW TREATMENT

Designing and creating new window treatments can represent a substantial investment of time and money and is an undertaking that deserves careful planning from the beginning. On the following pages are some guidelines to help you think through your design scheme and ensure that it will be a great success.

Before you buy any single component of your project, make sure all the necessary elements are available. If you are designing around a particular decorative rod, for example, don't buy the fabric to go with it until you're sure the manufacturer is still producing that style. And before you fall in love with a particular fabric, be sure the shop has, or can get, the yardage you will need.

If the new window treatment is just one aspect of a full-scale redecorating, decide upon all the separate elements before you actually begin any work. Find the paint color, the lampshade, the upholstery fabric, everything. This will help prevent a disappointment such as finding the most beautiful drapery fabric in the world just after you have painted the room—in a shade which doesn't quite go with it.

Allow enough time to do the job right. Many of us are stricken with an urge to redecorate just before the holidays or before the arrival of an old friend from college, but this probably is not the best time to schedule an elaborate new window treatment. Finding the right fabric or combination of fabrics may involve more than one shopping expedition. It may take several weeks to order fabric through a design studio. Measuring and figuring yardage requirements should not be rushed. And the sewing itself, while not complicated, will take time. If you give each step the time it requires, you will be happier with the results in the long run.

Involve other people in your household at the planning stage and demand that any Significant Other vote approval on your selection of style and fabric—beforehand. Your spouse may say "Oh, I don't care, honey, just get whatever you like," but after you've spent the year's decorating budget and four weeks making gorgeous mauve damask draperies for the dining room is not the time to learn that mauve gives him or her acute indigestion. Along this same vein, it is probably not a good idea to redecorate your teenage daughter's room to surprise her when she returns from summer camp.

Okay. You have decided upon a style you like, you've seen a wonderful fabric for it, and you've located every bit of trim and hardware to complete the design. Now close your eyes and try to visualize the finished project in your home.

Designing a window treatment involves both practical considerations and aesthetic decisions. Consider the practicalities first—these are the "givens" around which your design must work. The most beautiful window treatment in the world will not be a success if it doesn't meet your own needs in the area of usefulness. Check your design ideas against the list below before you make a final decision.

What will be the function of the window treatment?

Almost every drapery or curtain or swag or shade does—or can do—more than simply look beautiful at its window. Beyond its decorative aspect, think about the practical contributions your new treatment must make.

Privacy and security. Sheer curtains over the window during daylight hours will admit light yet restrict visibility from outside the house. A lined shade or draperies, or shutters, will provide nighttime privacy.

Light control. Most window treatments perform this function in one way or another, whether by closing out bright afternoon sun, or by allowing maximum light through the one small window of a room on the shady side of the house, or simply by diffusing and softening the light entering the room. Draperies which are easily drawn open and closed, opaque shades, and shutters all work well in this capacity.

Energy conservation. Effective window treatments can contribute a great deal toward lower heating and air conditioning bills. Draperies closed against the afternoon sun will keep a room several degrees cooler. White linings help further; they reflect light away from the window. Special reflective lining material, available through shops which sell decorator fabrics, is worth considering in a climate where cooling is a greater concern than heating. In this case, fabrics prone to sun fading are best avoided: Patterned linen, dark-colored cotton, or heavily dyed silk would not be good choices.

Almost any fabric covering a window will add some measure of warmth in winter. Heavier fabrics, of course, do more toward this end, and natural fiber fabrics generally are warmer than synthetics. Specially made thermal lining and/or interlining will insulate even better against cold that penetrates a window. If the window is drafty or the climate extremely cold, a Roman shade with thermal lining, fitted closely to the window glass, will provide excellent protection. In climates offering both extremes, a good bet is a separate thermal lining which can be hung behind the draperies during the winter and removed for summer.

Noise control. While it is an unimportant factor in most cases, even a single pair of draperies can greatly reduce the room's noise level. In a children's playroom, for example, which you may be tempted to decorate in such a way that it can be hosed down on a daily basis, an alternative might be ample curtains that can go into the washer and dryer.

Emphasizing or de-emphasizing a window. The fact that it's there doesn't mean it deserves the ultimate window treatment. A badly placed or strangely shaped window might call for plain draperies the color of the walls, which will de-emphasize the window and cause it to blend in with its surroundings. A shade or small curtain patterned to match the wallpaper makes a window seem to disappear.

If it's the only window in the room, or the view through it is spectacular, or it has an especially interesting shape, then you may want to use an elaborate top treatment, to give it a starring role in the decorating plan.

A softly draped swag will call attention to a window by altering its predictable rectangular shape. A simple wooden rod with a natural finish and plain stationary panels on either side can enhance a beautiful view without detracting from it.

Most window treatments serve more than one purpose, and your own plans may include functions not listed here. Whatever the practical role, it is an important consideration in planning.

■ What are the characteristics of the window?

The main consideration in choosing a style of treatment is probably the window itself: its size, its shape, the way it opens, and how it is situated in the room. Unless the window is never opened, allowance must be made for the movement of the

Long, graceful stationary panels subtly adorn the unusual window shape, yet do not detract from the view. Design: Kathryn Long.

sash and easy access to handles and locks. How will the proposed treatment look when the window is opened? It is easy to overlook this aspect of planning when the outside temperature is below freezing and you are sure spring will never come.

— ■ —

A wide window, such as this picture window, is a wonderful light source. A combination of sheers with draperies will diffuse strong sunlight and provide privacy. If the side windows will be opened, allow sufficient space at each side, when figuring rod length, so that draperies can clear the glass area completely. Longer rods will require intermediate supports to bear the weight of the draperies without sagging.

— ■ —

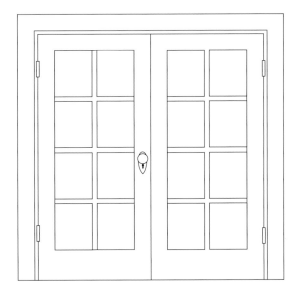

Sheer curtains covering just the glass of French doors are attractive and efficient when opacity is not required. Roller shades might also be installed at the top or at the bottom of each door. Draperies, on rods mounted above the doors or on the ceiling, provide maximum light control and privacy. Hems should be well weighted to keep the draperies in place when doors are opened and closed.

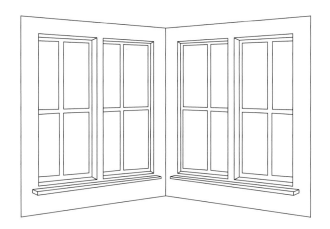

Windows in a group are fun to work with! An individual treatment can be made for each window, or the group can be handled as a unit. A combination treatment, such as a Roman shade at each window with a single top treatment above all four, allows better regulation of light. With the arrangement of windows shown here, rods with one-way draw would enable draperies to be opened from the corner outward to completely clear the glass area.

— ■ —

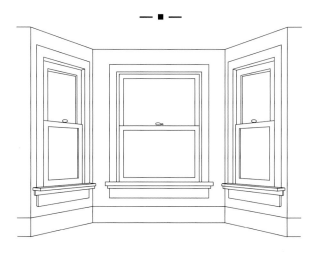

Bay windows can be treated as a group to emphasize the bay, or dressed separately to reduce the bay's prominence and scale. If the bay and the room are large enough, the bay windows might be decorated differently from those in the rest of the room, making the bay appear to be a separate room altogether. In cold weather, draperies hung from a ceiling-mounted rod across the bay opening can significantly reduce heat loss.

Dormer windows often provide less than adequate light, and care must be taken to be sure the curtains or shade can be opened to clear the glass area completely. A fabric shade works well if it can be mounted above the window, or draperies or curtains if there is room at the sides of the window for them to clear the glass. If the window is as wide as the recess, curtains might be hung from hinged rods which swing open to the sides of the recess.

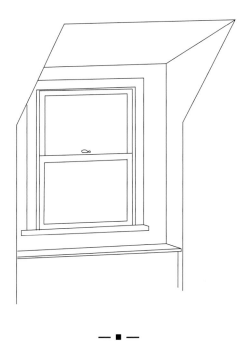

— ■ —

Ranch, or clerestory, windows are often placed above eye level and may call for special treatment to de-emphasize the short, wide configuration. Longer curtains might be attractive, or, space permitting, a valance could be placed above the window to add height. If privacy is not a factor, these windows might be left uncovered or have plain stationary panels at the sides for a clean, simple look.

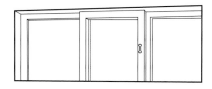

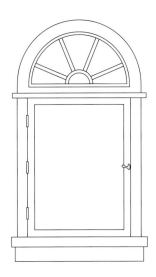

A bow window shares some characteristics with the bay window, page 11, but usually must be treated as a single window. For draperies, custom-made curved rods can be ordered through drapery suppliers. As with the bay window, a ceiling-mounted rod might be installed straight across the bow.

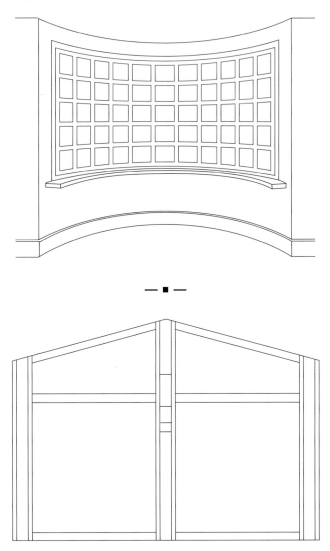

The fan light above a window is often left uncovered, unless privacy is an issue. A shaped sheer curtain above, combined with a curtain on the lower window as shown on page 77, covers the window without detracting from its attractive shape. If just the lower window is to be covered, a shade or curtain mounted inside the frame is best, as mounting a rod outside would alter the window's lines.

— ∎ —

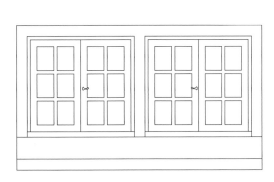

Casement windows, which open outward, require treatment which allows easy access to the windows. Draperies which can be drawn clear of the windows at the sides would work well. Fabric shades could be mounted on the frame above the windows and topped with a short valance. Curtains mounted inside the frame would be appropriate for the window style, and would serve nicely for windows that are rarely opened.

The upper section of a cathedral window often is left uncovered. If draperies or curtains are used for just the lower section, the rod should not extend beyond the sides of the frame or the vertical lines of the window will be distorted. If a rod is mounted above the apex of the window, a top treatment proportionate in length can lessen the effect of the draperies' long vertical lines.

A dual treatment enhances a two-story window.

— ■ —

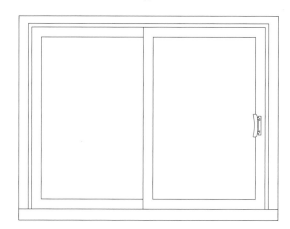

For sliding windows or glass doors, the main consideration is that draperies or curtains draw clear of the glass so they will not interfere with opening and closing, and won't get caught in the process. Weighted hems help keep draperies in place, as will decorative holdbacks mounted at the sides of the windows. A top treatment, also designed to stay out of the way, can soften the rather stark lines of this window style.

■ What is the function of the room?

How the room is used will affect the choice of both style and materials for your window treatment. An infrequently used living room might be the place to indulge your secret desire for eggshell silk shades. For a family room where all the neighborhood teenagers convene, washable curtains are worth considering, perhaps in a color that goes well with pizza sauce. Remember that prints and patterns are less likely to show spots than are very dark or very light solids. For the kitchen and bathrooms, washable window treatments, in fabrics not affected by steam, are a good choice. Fairly temporary treatments may suit children's rooms, so they can be updated to keep pace with a child's ever-changing preferences.

Don't forget the pets. Cat won't think twice about slipping between the new curtains to get to her favorite sunny window sill, leaving fur-trimmed edges in her wake. And elegant long draperies that puddle on the floor may provide an ideal place for the beagle to nap.

■ What is the style of the room — and of its occupants?

If you are working with a Victorian restoration, a new beach cottage, or an ultra-modern apartment, you already have some guidelines as to style and design for your window treatments. Many of us live happily with eclectic decorating schemes, but mixing styles has to be done carefully to avoid results that look more odd than interesting.

Is the room especially masculine or feminine? Are you trying to achieve a restful atmosphere in a bedroom, a cozy feeling for a den, or something to soften the rather functional lines of a workroom? The style of treatment you choose can greatly alter the style of the room.

Personal style, too, affects your choices. Does your home always look as if you are expecting the pho-

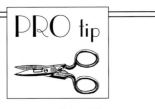
tography team for a decorating magazine at any moment? Or do you get around to serious cleaning every time the weekend has a second Saturday? Consider whether your proposed window treatment is going to be fussy about care and, if so, whether you want to give it the extra time.

▪ What other furnishings do you have to work with?

If you're starting with a bare room, lucky you! In most cases there is furniture or a rug or some element in the room with which a new window treatment must be compatible. First, be certain you are designing around this thing because you want to do so, not just because you have it, because there's nothing really wrong with it (except that you've never liked it), or because it was Grandmother's. This may be

An innovative design for controlling light, a tab-top curtain on the upper bed frame slides along just far enough to keep bright morning sun from sleepy eyes. On the window itself is a simple valance trimmed with Battenberg lace. A pleasant mix of print fabrics gives the room a well-coordinated look.
Design: Donna Evans

the time to take a deep breath and put an ad in the paper. Someone, somewhere, will love that thing as much as Grandmother did.

■ How much time and money do you have?

It's terribly unfair that budget can have veto power over a fabulous design, but it is better to know in advance what you're up against. Most window treatments require substantial yardage, and what seems a reasonable per-yard price for fabric can quickly multiply into an unaffordable pair of draperies. In the interest of working within the budget, it is helpful to add up the cost of the underpinnings—the hardware, lining, heading tape, and so forth—before you select a decorator fabric.

Consider long-term value as well as immediate cost. How long will you keep this window treatment? The ill-fitting, wrong-colored temporary curtains you buy just to have something over the windows will probably outlive your grandchildren. If you are renting and plan to buy a home soon, you won't want window treatments that cost more than your lease; they will not fit the new house. Balance the expenditure against the proposed life of the treatment.

Beware of false economy. Deciding to forgo lining in order to buy a more expensive face fabric (the one that shows) will result in cheap-looking draperies even with the good decorator fabric. Designers and professional installers all caution against trying to save money by re-using old rods that are not quite right for the new treatment. A bargain fabric may not have the finish or stability necessary for the project you plan. And, most important, don't try to save on the quantity when you buy fabric. Draperies with skimpy hems or with panels that are too narrow will never look quite right, regardless of the fabric quality. And failure to allow enough material for matching a print can mean buying another entire panel—if the fabric is still available.

There *are* ways to save money. There are real fabric bargains to be found with careful shopping. Some treatment styles take less fabric than others; you might consider using an expensive fabric in Roman shades instead of draperies, or making a simple valance for the top instead of a yardage-consuming swag. And remember that you are saving money—a considerable amount of it—by making your own window treatments in the first place.

■ Designing Your Window Treatment ■

Once you are aware of the practical requirements and other factors that have to be taken into consideration, you can move on to the exciting part of your planning—working with styles, colors, and fabrics. All these elements must work in harmony to create an effective window treatment.

■ Choosing a Style

The color photographs offer a wonderful array of styles for every kind of decor. Other books and magazines can provide hundreds of additional ideas. Look at your friends' homes. Visit public places:

Historic homes, museums, restaurants, and hotels can all give you ideas. Yes, they probably have more extensive decorating budgets than yours, and their window treatments may be a bit elaborate for the mountain cabin you're living in, but if you look closely at what these places have done, most likely with the help of professional designers, you may find wonderful details that you can incorporate into your plans—an interesting way of pleating a drapery heading, an unusual tieback, an innovative use for cording.

Keep your room size in mind when you are considering styles, especially if you are looking at pho-

tographs. The magazine photo of an elaborate treatment may not indicate the room's 20-foot ceilings;
such a treatment might be all out of proportion for
your home. Or delicate ruffle-trimmed curtains, beautiful in a picture, might be too small in scale for your
large master bedroom.

Most of all, be creative. Combine ideas from different sources, and don't restrict yourself to what
you've seen of other people's designs. Even if you
do find a photograph or living example of precisely
what you want, you could spend the rest of your life
searching for that exact fabric. Give yourself some
leeway with your design. And experiment!

▪ Fabrics

The main component of most window treatments is
fabric. When you set out to design your own window treatment, chances are that you envision a fabric, or look for a fabric, before you do anything else.
The next chapter contains much information about
fabric characteristics, and you need to know
whether your fabric of choice has the qualities to
make it suitable for the treatment style you are considering.

▪ Colors

The most important single element of your overall
design is the color you choose. You are probably
familiar with some of the ways color can change a
room: adding bright yellow to cheer up a gray room
on the north side of the house, adding blues and
greens to subdue incoming sun on the west side, or
introducing a bit of coral to an all-neutral room to
bring it to life.

The effects of color are not always so predictable.
It is possible to hang draperies in your favorite shade
of blue and be totally disappointed with the result,
perhaps because of the way the blue interacts with
furniture colors, or because of the way the light from
the window affects the blue, or because that particular blue is your favorite only in small doses after all.

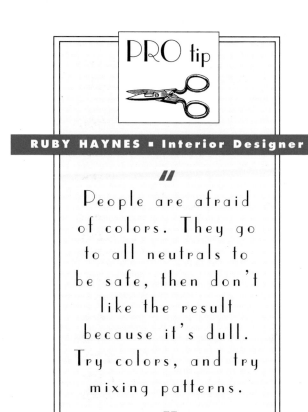

Colors which you enjoy wearing may not please you
as part of a decorating scheme.

Combinations of colors can also surprise. Two
which blend beautifully when you look at small
swatches may clash violently in large quantities. Or
a color you never dreamed of using may prove to
be a perfect accent to tie the whole plan together.
When you are trying to coordinate a solid with a
print, stand back and look at the combination from
the distance at which you'll see the window treatment. The solid may exactly match one of the colors
in the print yet fail to blend with the pattern as a
whole once you back up a few feet. Take samples
of every color in the room when you shop, including
the wood colors of the furniture. In the store, walk
them past even unlikely fabrics just to see what happens.

Colors affect us all in different, and sometimes
subtle, ways. You may be aware that red causes
you to burst into song and violet makes you queasy,
but have you ever been in a room that simply made

you uncomfortable for no apparent reason? It could be the color. Enlightening books have been written about the psychology of color; one of them might help you with a choice. Do experiment! If you are working around a gray sofa, but spending time in the presence of gray depresses you, find a color for your window treatment that will overpower the gray or will change it.

Once you have decided or nearly decided upon a color or color combination, it is very important to look at a large piece of the proposed selection in the room where it will be used. Buy a yard or two, bring it home and look to see that it blends with the other furnishings under all possible lighting situations. Look at it in sunny daylight, gray daylight, and at night with the lamps on. Certain colors—especially greens and beiges, for some reason—change drastically with changes in the lighting. Sheer curtains will look very different against the window at night than with the morning sun shining through them.

Your preferences are more important in the long run than sticking to a color scheme. Take the time to make certain you can live happily ever after with the colors you choose.

■ Patterns

The choice of pattern will greatly affect the look of your chosen style. The same style draperies and valance made up in bright striped fabric would look altogether different in a random floral print or a nubby-textured neutral color.

With patterned fabric, it is important that the pattern suit the size of the window and of the room. A small print, appealing at close range, disappears completely in floor-length draperies at a moderately large window. From across the room, it will merge into a solid color—one you wouldn't have chosen. A print which, up close, is outrageously large and bold may be exactly right for that window. Small rooms call for scaled-down patterns. A large print will look even larger in a tiny powder room, and long

draperies with bold vertical stripes will give you the feeling of being in an elevator shaft.

Mixing patterns requires a careful eye, some study, and a great deal of trial and error. A seemingly random assortment of patterns and textures in a flawlessly decorated room is no accident, but the result of planning and experimentation. There is no list of rules to follow; you must depend on your eye and trust your own good judgment. If you put a combination of patterns together and your immediate reaction is Yes! then you should go with it. If you still can't decide after looking at it for a reasonable length of time, or if your opinion wavers, then it's probably best to try something else.

Work toward a balance. You may want one element of the room to overpower all others, and a bold print can achieve that result. For an evenly balanced look, no one pattern should be dominant. Decorator fabrics are often available as "families," with several complementary patterns in a single color scheme.

As with color, it is important to choose patterns that please you. If large floral prints make you twitchy, don't use them! There are plenty of alternatives.

■ Textures

A variety of fabric textures in a room can be as interesting as a combination of patterns, and the addition of a different texture can have the same impact as the addition of a new color. If your room is full of nubby-textured upholstery, try a corded fabric for the window treatment. Or consider a plain, smooth cotton with an oriental rug. Texture combinations require the same experimentation and careful testing that patterns do.

■ Trims

There are magnificent cords, braids, tassels, and fringes available from the manufacturers of decorator fabrics. Some are made to coordinate with particular fabrics; others are more generic. Trims can be very effective when considered as an element of the original design. A thick cord below the heading on plain draperies can give them a much more elegant look. A narrow fringe at the inner and lower edges can add a little color without confusing the design plan. Trims, too, should be compatible with the other fabrics and features of the room.

▪ H a r d w a r e

If you haven't made window treatments in some time, you are going to be very surprised to see what has happened to drapery rods, brackets, hooks, rings, and all the other necessary support materials. Your design is not restricted to a few basic rod styles of hardware; there is hardware available to complement the most extraordinary design you can contrive, whatever the shape and size of your window.

Many decorative rods and brackets are design elements in themselves. A thick wooden rod and rings, perhaps painted or given a faux finish, can coordinate with the fabric you've chosen, or can add a completely different color and texture. Ornamental brackets will transform a plain scarf into a complete window treatment. Nor are you restricted to hardware made specifically for curtains. There are wonderful drapery rods made of PVC plumbing pipe and beautiful swags draped over brass coat hooks! Your creativity should serve you well in this area, too, but do remember that the most important function of the hardware is to hold up all that fabric.

There is more information about strictly functional hardware in the chapter on Materials. If you are considering the decorative variety, though, it should be part of your design plan from the beginning.

Imaginative hardware, such as the brass bathroom tissue holders in the center, can play an important role.

W h e n   t o   C a l l   i n   t h e   P r o s

If by now the whole project has you completely stymied, or if you just can't decide what color or style will work best, or if you aren't sure your great ideas are so great after all, perhaps it's time to seek out a specialist. Professional interior designers can help in several ways. They have encountered every conceivable set of circumstances, and your insurmountable problem most likely is one they have solved many times. They understand the effects of colors, they are experienced at combining patterns, they are on working with terms with thousands of different fabrics and

know which are most suitable for any given style of window treatment. Many of them are imaginative and creative, and the good ones will listen to you.

Most designers will consult with you for an hourly fee even if you are doing the work yourself. A designer can save you money by making sure your fabric is appropriate for your chosen style of treatment and by taking accurate measurements. If you order fabric through a design studio (most do not stock fabrics), you will get a good bit of knowledgeable advice at no extra charge.

How do you locate a good designer? Call friends who have worked with designers, and call the historic homes, restaurants, or hotels whose decorating schemes impressed you when you were looking for ideas. Or you might check with the local branch of the trade association, the American Society of Interior Designers, which regulates the profession to some extent. To qualify as a professional member of the ASID, a designer must have a combination of formal education and experience in the field and must pass a rigorous examination.

▪ Window Shopping ▪

Devote some time to preparation before you go out to buy the materials for your project. Read the sections on measurements (page 43), fabrics (page 22), and hardware (page 35) before you shop.

Measure the windows. These measurements will give you the approximate finished dimensions for your treatment, which you will need in order to buy rods and to determine fabric yardage requirements after pattern matching and other variables are figured. Make photocopies of the window diagram on page 43, one for each window, and add them to your shopping kit. They will help you visualize the fabric actually on your windows.

Write out your requirements. Take along a checklist of the factors which you have to consider. You'll be able to eliminate many choices immediately.

Assemble a kit for shopping trips. To help with matching, take paint chips, swatches of other fabrics in the room, a scrap of carpet, and pillow covers. If you don't have samples of the fabrics, take another piece of fabric in the same color, or pick up paint chips in those colors. Take the largest samples you can find; a single loop of carpet yarn cut from the corner won't tell you much.

Take your annotated window diagrams and your checklist. Include a tape measure and, above all, a calculator.

▪ C a r e & C l e a n i n g ▪

It may seem premature to discuss maintenance at this point in the game, but you might want to give a thought to cleaning at the planning stage. You'll probably invest considerable time in your window treatments. What can you do to ensure that they have a long and happy life?

Most professional designers suggest regular vacuuming, with the vacuum cleaner at the lowest suction setting, as the best possible care for a window treatment. Vacuuming removes dust and pollen that cause allergy problems for some people and eventually affect the fabric.

Periodic airing helps keep them fresh, too. Take them outside on a dry, breezy October day and hang them on the clothesline or porch railing for the afternoon.

Dry cleaning may be necessary sooner or later, and the designers say later is better. The finishes added to many of the decorator fabrics are removed to some extent in the dry cleaning process, leaving the fabric less crisp, and without some of the protection against stains or sun that the finishes provide.

Use a reputable dry cleaner. (Why do instructions always say that? As if you would willingly seek out the other kind!) Check with friends or decorators or

drapery supply stores for recommendations.

The dry cleaner, of course, is often working blind. There are so many different fabrics and fabric finishes, all with different care requirements, that without knowledge of the specifics the cleaner has to guess at the best way to deal with your fabric. Keep information as to fiber content, finishes, and manufacturer's care suggestions so you can give this information to the cleaner when the time comes. By doing so you will also protect yourself, in case there are problems.

Much of the care for your window treatment happens before you even begin to sew. Many curtains and draperies can be washed if you choose appropriate fabrics and preshrink them. If you can, resist buying fabric strictly for color or pattern, and consider the physical situation in which your draperies will hang. Choose light-colored fabric for sunny south-facing windows, and washable fabric for the room with the wood stove.

There also is the question of how long you really want the window treatment to last. There may come a time when you just want something different. If the draperies have been there for 10 years and still show no symptoms of aging, it is difficult to find an excuse to replace them.

MATERIALS

Whatever the style of their window treatments, people who end up happy with their completed projects have done at least two things right: They've found appropriate fabric and they've found functional hardware.

▪ F a b r i c ▪

The main component of most window treatments is fabric, and selecting and shopping for your fabric can be the most exciting—and the most challenging—aspect of your project. The assortment of fabrics out there is staggering! It's best to start out with some idea of what you want, but also with a little flexibility in your design scheme, just in case you can't find the linen with the half-inch gold stripe that exactly matches the gold on the pillow that Mom made with a cream background that exactly matches the cream of the mat on the print that you bought in Montreal.

It is important to have some understanding of fabrics and their characteristics so you can be fairly sure that the fabric whose appearance appeals to you will also fulfill the purpose you have in mind for it. A window treatment project often requires many yards of fabric, and buying a large quantity of cloth which later proves unsuitable can be a costly mistake.

Every last piece of fabric in the world has a personality of its own. Each one has a unique "hand," or feel. Each will drape in a particular manner, respond differently to laundering or dry cleaning, and adapt in its own way to hanging in front of a window for several years. If you have some knowledge of fabrics and the fibers of which they are composed, you will be better equipped to select a fabric which will serve you well.

▪ T r a d e T a l k

Fabric has its own language. It is helpful to know the terms used to describe the components and qualities of fabrics.

Bias is the diagonal of a piece of fabric. True bias follows a line exactly halfway between the lengthwise and crosswise grains, or a 45-degree angle. When used as a verb, bias refers to the tendency of some fabrics to torque so that their lengthwise and crosswise grainlines are not perpendicular to one another. Fabrics stretch considerably more on the bias than on the straight grainlines.

Grain of fabric is the direction of the threads.

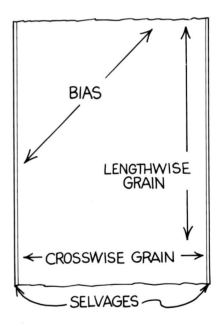

Lengthwise grain refers to the threads in a fabric which lie parallel to the selvage edges. Most fabrics stretch least along the lengthwise grain.

Crosswise grain refers to the threads which are perpendicular to the selvage edges. Most fabrics have more stretch along the crosswise grain than lengthwise.

Hand simply means the feel of the fabric.

Knit fabrics are made by an interlocking series of yarn loops. Knits are characterized by stretchiness and may exhibit a "run" at the point where a thread is cut.

Mercerization is a process used on cotton to increase its luster. The process also increases the fiber's ability to hold dye.

Nap is surface pile or "hairiness" which lies in one direction on the fabric, as on panne velvet or corduroy. When cutting napped fabrics, be careful to cut all pieces in the same direction.

Pile is made up of yarns which project from the face of the fabric, such as on velvet.

Repeat of a pattern, printed or woven, refers to the space occupied by a completed pattern. For window treatments the lengthwise pattern repeat—which often is 27"—must be taken into consideration when determining yardage requirements. The horizontal repeat is less important, but affects matching at seamlines and positioning some top treatments.

Selvage, or selvedge, is the finished outer edge on each side of the fabric.

Sizing is a finishing compound applied to fabric to give it smoothness, stiffness, stability, or sheen. Sizing is removed through laundering or dry cleaning. Abrasion and wear will also reduce its effects.

Warp refers to the threads in woven fabric which comprise the lengthwise grain and are parallel to the selvages.

Weft refers to the crosswise fibers in woven fabric, those perpendicular to the selvages and to the lengthwise grain.

Woven fabric is made up of interlaced yarns or threads. Generally, it consists of lengthwise threads, or warp; and crosswise threads, called weft, or filler.

▪ What You Need to Know About Fibers

Fibers are the raw materials from which fabrics are made.

Each different fiber has its own unique qualities, so it is important to know the fiber content of the fabrics you buy. Fiber content will determine how the fabric will behave during construction and pressing, how it will hang and drape, and what kind of care the finished product will demand.

Reputable fabric suppliers label their goods as to fiber content and will be able to supply manufacturer's care instructions. Discount stores and mill ends stores, which stock manufacturers' overruns and seconds, can be a source for great bargains, but they may not be able to provide fiber content or care information for the piece you select.

Fibers from which fabrics are made are classified either as natural or man-made, according to their origin. Natural fibers are those which originate from plants and animals—cotton, linen, ramie, silk, and wool. Man-made (or synthetic) fibers, such as polyester, nylon, and acrylic, are made from chemical compounds. A "blend" can be any combination of fibers making up a fabric but most often refers to the combination of a natural fiber with a synthetic.

Below are descriptions of the fibers from which fabrics are created. Think of their characteristics when planning your project; when you are ready to shop you'll know what kind of fabric will be most suitable.

The Naturals

Fabrics made from natural fibers have aesthetic qualities which cannot be duplicated synthetically. What can compare with the subtle luster of silk peau de soie, or the rich, muted colors of a paisley-printed wool challis, or the smoothness of fine pima cotton, or the soft, nubby texture of an antique piece of linen?

Generally speaking, natural-fiber fabrics are easier to work with than synthetics. They are obedient: Most can be creased with the fingers, a great time-saver on a project requiring miles of hems. Most of them respond to shaping, at least to some extent. Natural fibers are more absorbent than synthetics, a trait which makes them comfortable to wear but which can cause draperies to stretch in length in humid weather unless the fabric is treated to be moisture resistant.

Virtually all natural-fiber fabrics are washable, and nearly all will shrink in the process. The fabrics must be preshrunk if they are to be used in garments or other items that will later be washed. Washing also will remove the finishes used, particularly on heavier silks.

They appeal to the purists among us. Unfortunately, many provide a food source for certain moths and for dermestid beetles.

Cotton is the most versatile of all fabrics for home decorating. It is available in a vast range of weaves and finishes. It is durable, takes dyes well, and requires a minimum of care. Somewhere there is a cotton fabric guaranteed to enhance any style of decor.

To give them smoothness and stability, lower-end cottons often are treated with a finishing agent such as starch. The finish washes out, leaving the fabric softer, less smooth, and with less body. Dry cleaning prolongs the life of the finish, particularly with fabrics manufactured specifically for decorating.

The suitability of cotton fabric for a window treatment depends upon the weight, weave, and finish of the fabric and upon the style of the treatment. A soft, loosely woven cotton would work beautifully as a scarf or swag, for example, but would stretch and sag if used in floor-length draperies.

Linen is an extremely strong and durable fabric. The fibers undergo a complex process in their transition from plant to fabric, which accounts for linen's

relatively high price.

Linen ages gracefully; the more it is used and laundered, the softer and more lustrous it becomes. White or natural colored linens can withstand washing in hot water with bleach, but dyed linens should be treated more gently to keep their colors from fading. Linen will wrinkle. It's that quality which separates the real thing from the imitations. Even with wrinkles, linen has a distinctive and handsome appearance no synthetic can match.

Linen is available in a number of different weaves and textures, but is most often seen in a slightly nubby plain weave—the characteristic "linen weave" we associate with the fabric. Linen is the *fiber*, however, not the weave. There is no such thing as "synthetic linen."

Ramie also is a plant fiber. It produces a fabric similar to linen but somewhat coarser, not quite as durable, and less costly. It can be treated in the same way as linen or cotton, and usually is blended with one or the other in fabrics. Ramie is in no way related to rayon, by the way.

Silk fibers produce fabrics which are unsurpassed for elegance and luxurious appearance. Many silk fabrics have an inherent stiffness which allows them to drape and fold in a distinctive way. Some are very soft and light, and others are rough-textured and heavy.

Lighter-weight silks wash beautifully, although they shrink. Heavy silks and heavily dyed silks should be dry-cleaned. Silks also are prone to sun-fading; dyed silk used for window treatments should always be lined. when you are ready to shop you'll know what kind of fabric will be most suitable.

Wool fibers produce fabric which takes dye extremely well and is a remarkable insulator. It can be shaped and molded with ease. It is available in many different weaves and finishes. Wool is not commonly used for home decorating—it is fairly expensive—but can be very elegant for draperies and upholstery.

Contrary to popular belief, most woolens wash beautifully. Wool must be preshrunk before sewing if the finished product will be laundered. It should be washed in cool or tepid water, as either extremely hot or extremely cold water will cause the fibers to mat, and it should be washed with soap, not detergent.

Synthetic Fibers

In general, fabrics made from synthetic fibers are washable and resist wrinkling. They hold color well, and they are impervious to insect damage. Most synthetic fabrics are quite stable—they don't tend to stretch out of shape, which also means that they have little "ease" and cannot be shaped and molded as natural fiber fabrics can. Most synthetics are less expensive than their natural-fiber counterparts.

Changes and improvements in synthetic fibers occur hourly, and for this reason it is especially important with synthetic fabrics to follow manufacturers' guidelines for washing or dry cleaning and pressing. Some are sensitive to heat and will pucker or melt with the touch of a too-hot iron. Some will yellow if washed with chlorine bleach. Others are affected by certain chemicals: Nail polish remover will dissolve acetate. But for the most part synthetics are very easy to care for—it's just a matter of following their instructions.

Polyester is probably the most widely used man-made fiber. It is extremely durable, and it is available in every conceivable weave and texture. Polyester fabrics wash well, with little or no shrinkage, and dry quickly. They resent chlorine bleach—it will yellow a white fabric—and too hot an iron may cause puckering or shrinking. They retain their shape and resist fading. Static electricity can be a problem in dry winter weather, but the condition can be alleviated by the use of a fabric softener when laundering, or with an anti-static spray.

Polyester often is blended with natural fibers to give them strength and stability. The resulting blends are often less expensive and easier to care for than the comparable natural-fiber fabrics. Cotton/polyester blends are a good choice for curtains and draperies, and many decorator fabrics have this fiber content. Polyester/linen blends wrinkle less than pure linen—and usually are much less expensive. Combined with wool, polyester adds stability and usually produces a less expensive fabric.

Acetate is a man-made fiber derived from cellulose. It has a silky look and feel, and it drapes well. Some acetate fabrics will wrinkle, and some are susceptible to sun-fading. Acetate is often blended with cotton to produce taffeta and faille fabrics with a beautiful sheen. Fabrics containing acetate nearly always should be dry cleaned.

Acrylic, a synthetic fiber, produces a soft, woolly fabric. It launders well, and it resists wrinkles and sunlight. Acrylic fabrics are quite stable—they don't tend to stretch or sag—but they also don't have the "memory" of wool. Acrylics can be dyed in very vivid colors, which is one way to distinguish acrylic fabrics from the woolen fabrics they resemble. Acrylic often is blended with wool to produce a less costly fabric.

Nylon was the original synthetic fiber. Strong, resistant to mildew and rot, it launders easily, dries quickly, and requires little in the way of ironing. Fabrics for making sheer curtains sometimes are nylon, but nylon is more often found in knit fabrics and in the high-tech fabrics used for outdoor wear and the like.

Rayon is somewhat of a hybrid, a man-made fiber from a natural substance. Like acetate, rayon is made of cellulose but by a different process. Rayon fabrics are very soft and fluid and have an attractive sheen. Rayon is not strong, and it does not hold its shape well. It is often combined with fabrics which are stronger and more stable, such as cotton or polyester, giving them the benefit of its excellent draping qualities. Most rayons and rayon blends should be dry cleaned.

Blends

A "blend" of course can be any combination of fibers making up a fabric. The term is most often used, though, to refer to a combination of a natural fiber with a synthetic to produce a fabric which has the stability and ease of care of the synthetic, and the aesthetic appeal of the natural fiber fabric. So a "cotton blend" could be linen and cotton, but is more likely cotton and polyester, or cotton and rayon.

▪ Fabrics

A fabric is identified by the fiber from which it is made, by its weave structure, by its design or patterning, and by its surface finish. All these characteristics need to be considered when a fabric is selected for a window treatment. Each fiber, each finish, and every conceivable combination of fiber and weave produces a fabric with its own unique characteristics. Understanding the qualities of different fabrics will help you decide which will best suit your purpose.

It is the weave structure that often defines the fabric. A piece of woven fabric is made up of *warp* threads, those which are parallel to the selvage (the finished edge); and the *weft*, or filler, which is the threads running perpendicular to the warp and selvage. The warp threads constitute the lengthwise grain of the fabric; the weft, the crosswise grain.

Knit fabrics—all those which are not woven—are wonderful things, but the soft, stretchy quality that makes them so pleasant to wear also makes them fairly unsuitable for window treatments—unless you're trying for something way out of the ordinary.

The weave structures of woven fabrics can be divided into three general categories. *Plain weave*, the most basic, is the structure of most fabrics. It is a simple over-and-under weave, with the warp and

weft threads usually of about the same thickness. *Twill weave* produces a durable fabric with a distinctive diagonal rib. Gabardine is a twill weave; the herringbone pattern is a variation of a twill weave. *Satin weave* is characterized by a great number of "floats" on the face of the fabric—weft threads (usually) which are not interwoven with the warp over specified intervals. Satin weave fabrics have a distinctive smooth appearance.

To describe all the weaves, structures, textures, and finishes that turn fibers into fabrics would fill several books this size. Those included below are fabrics which would work well for one kind of window treatment or another, and which are widely available.

Batiste is a lightweight, soft, sheer fabric, usually of cotton or cotton/polyester blend, but also available in silk.

Broadcloth is a tightly woven, smoothly finished fabric. It can be made of virtually any fiber, but the term most often refers to cotton or cotton/polyester blend fabrics.

Brocade fabric is rich and heavy, with a jacquard pattern woven in the background color or different colors. The pattern may be a different weave than the background, or woven with different yarns, giving texture and dimension to the fabric. Silk, wool, rayon, cotton, and blends are used for brocades.

Buckram is a coarse, heavily sized fabric used primarily for stiffening. It may be made of cotton and polyester or other fibers. It is usually sold in narrow widths, sometimes as two layers glued together, and is available with a fusible backing.

Calico, a lightweight, plain weave cloth, is characterized by its small figured prints. Calico usually is cotton, but may be a cotton blend

Canvas covers a broad range of sturdy, plain weave fabrics, usually cotton or cotton with polyester. *Duck* and *sailcloth* are lighter weight fabrics in the same category.

Chambray is a plain weave, yarn-dyed cotton or cotton blend fabric with colored warp and white weft, or filler.

China silk is a fine, lightweight silk. It is most often found in solid colors and is a beautiful choice for sheer curtains.

Chintz is characterized by its crispness and sheen. It is a plain weave cotton or cotton blend fabric, usually in solid colors, floral prints, or stripes. Its glazed finish wears off with abrasion and repeated dry cleaning. Laundering removes the finish altogether.

Crinoline is a very stiff open-weave fabric of varying fiber content. It is heavily sized and is available in narrow widths for use as a stiffener for drapery headings.

Damask is nearly always a solid color fabric, with a pattern or design in satin weave against a plain weave background. Damask can be cotton, silk, linen, wool, a combination of these fibers, or a blend of one of these with a synthetic.

Dotted Swiss is a sheer, soft, usually white fabric with a regular overall pattern of small dots, which traditionally were woven into the fabric but are now applied to the surface. Most dotted Swiss now available is cotton/polyester blend. All-cotton dotted Swiss can be located with some effort; it is incredibly beautiful and priced accordingly!

Eyelet is a form of embroidery in which designs are cut out of the fabric and their edges finished with an overcast stitch. Machine-made eyelet is usually of a cotton/polyester blend, and is available in trims of varying width or in standard fabric widths

Faille is a plain weave fabric with a narrow horizontal rib, now usually rayon or rayon and cotton, although silk and wool faille is available. Faille can be soft or slightly crisp, depending on the fiber content. It is sometimes embossed with moiré patterning.

Flannel is a soft, plain or twill weave fabric with a slight nap, valued for its warmth. Flannel is usually made of wool, but may be cotton—in which case it is called *flannelette*—rayon, or acrylic.

Gabardine, a smooth, twill weave fabric with a distinctive diagonal rib, can be wool, rayon, silk, or blends of any of these fibers with a synthetic. Gabardine resists wrinkling and has good draping qualities.

Ikat is a design technique developed in northeastern Asia. The yarns are tie-dyed before weaving, producing a distinctive pattern in the cloth. Ikat fabrics are usually cotton or silk.

Indian cotton is a general term for fabric produced in India from the locally grown short fiber cottons. It is lightweight and soft, often heavily sized for stability. *Madras*, from that region of India, is colored with vegetable dyes that are intended to bleed. Plaid and striped patterns are most often associated with Madras.

Jacquard is a weaving process by which patterns can be woven into the cloth with different colors or types of yarn, and with a different weave structure used for the patterning. Damask is a jacquard-woven fabric. Jacquard fabrics can be of virtually any fiber content.

Lace refers to delicate openwork fabrics which incorporate a design into a meshlike background. There are hundreds of lacemaking techniques and traditions. The readily available laces are machine made, therefore affordable. The wider machine-made laces which might be used for window treatments are usually made with at least some polyester or other synthetic, as natural fiber laces of this size would not retain their shape.

Lawn is a smooth, lightweight, plain weave fabric slightly heavier than batiste. It is usually associated with cotton fabric, but it can be made of linen or of cotton/polyester blend

Moiré is a rippling watermark pattern embossed onto the fabric with rollers. Moiré patterning works best on fabrics with a woven horizontal rib: silk, cotton, acetate, rayon, or blends of those fibers. Cotton and other fabrics are sometimes printed with a pattern resembling moiré.

Muslin is a basic, homey, light to medium weight cotton or cotton/polyester fabric usually found in natural (unbleached) color or white. It is very inexpensive and is useful for many home-decorating projects, especially in a behind-the-scenes capacity.

Organdy is a fine, sheer, somewhat stiff cotton fabric. Much of its crispness is due to the tight twist of the yarns rather than to the added sizing and is thus retained after laundering.

Peau de Soie is silk, strictly speaking, a heavyweight fabric of satin weave with a fine horizontal rib. The term now is commonly used for similar synthetic fabrics.

Pima cotton, also known as Egyptian cotton, is the long staple cotton grown in, or originating in, Egypt. It is used to make fine, high quality cotton fabric with a silky hand. Pima cotton is a variety of Egyptian cotton which is grown in the southwestern United States.

Piqué fabrics feature raised woven patterns such as cord, waffle, or bird's eye. Piqué fabrics are light to medium weight, usually cotton, rayon, or one of the two blended with polyester. Piqué is woven in white or a solid color but may be printed.

Plaid commonly refers to a pattern of vertical and horizontal interwoven stripes of different colors. Strictly speaking, such patterns are *tartans*. Plaid is an old term which originally meant a length of tartan cloth as it came off the loom.

Polished cotton is a cotton fabric which is finished with starch or wax to give it sheen and crispness. The finish is not washable, but will last through several dry cleanings.

Satin is one of the basic weave structures as well as the name of fabrics woven with that structure. Satin fabrics have a characteristic sheen which is a function of the weave, not of finishing agents, so is not removed by washing or dry cleaning. Satin fabric usually is made of the more lustrous fibers: silk, rayon, cotton, wool, and some synthetics. Satin-weave cotton is called sateen.

Sea Island cotton, considered the finest cotton available, produces a beautiful silky fabric. It is cultivated on islands off the Georgia and South Carolina coasts, and in the West Indies.

Sheeting is a broad category which includes a variety of wide-loomed cotton or cotton/polyester fabrics, most often unbleached or white, or in solid colors.

Taffeta is a finely woven, light to medium weight fabric with a crisp finish and a fine horizontal rib. It has a fairly high sheen or a dull sheen; in the latter case it is called "antique taffeta." Taffeta can be a silk fabric, but is more often made of rayon or rayon and cotton, or of other synthetics. Taffeta is sometimes used for moiré patterning.

Tapestry is a heavy woven fabric which often depicts historic scenes and floral patterns. It is most commonly available in cotton, wool, and cotton/rayon blends.

Thai silk (from Thailand, of course) is a plain weave, lightweight silk, usually in bright colors or with a woven plaid pattern.

Twill is one of the basic weave structures, and also the name given to fabrics woven in that manner. Twills generally are quite sturdy, and when made of a softer fiber, such as rayon, may have excellent drapability as well.

Velvet is a rich fabric with a cut pile surface. It may have a lustrous or dull surface, and it may be rather stiff or very soft and drapable, depending upon its fiber content. Originally always silk, velvet now is also made of rayon, a blend of silk and rayon, cotton, or wool. Cotton velvet is often called *velveteen*. Cotton and cotton/polyester velvets may be washable, and some can even be machine dried with success. Other velvets should be dry cleaned.

Voile is a sheer, lightweight fabric with some crispness. It has a rather loose weave, but is fairly stable because of the tight twist of the yarns with which it is woven. The fiber content is most often cotton or a cotton/polyester blend.

▪ Decorator Fabrics Versus Fashion Fabrics

There are some important differences between fabrics manufactured for use in home decorating and those intended for use in garment construction.

Decorator fabrics are most often woven in 54" widths. This is an advantage with window treatments because a curtain or panel for a standard window can be made from one width of fabric, eliminating the need for piecing.

Decorator fabrics are given different finishes from fabrics meant to be worn next to the body. They are treated to make them repel soil, stains, and moisture, and to help them resist mildew and fading. Some are given a flame-retardant finish. The finishing process also gives added stability to the fabric so that even a weighty length, such as in floor-length draperies, can hang for a long time without sagging or stretching out of shape. The finish also may give the fabric, cotton especially, an attractive surface sheen.

Adding these desirable qualities to a fabric also adds to its cost, which is one reason a decorator fabric is priced somewhat higher than a similar fashion fabric. The finish also will extend the life of the fabric and help it better perform the rather difficult task you plan for it.

Washing removes many of the finishing agents used with decorator fabrics. They will last somewhat longer with dry cleaning.

All this does not exclude fashion fabrics altogether from your decorating plans. Some fabrics, in some cases, can be absolutely fabulous. A delicate gingham check might be just the thing for light curtains in the kitchen; a cotton print featuring dinosaurs or jungle creatures could brighten a child's bedroom; wool in the family's own ancestral tartan would make distinctive draperies for a den. But unless you are familiar with the characteristics of the fabric under consideration and feel certain it will perform as you wish, it is probably safest to stick with those fabrics intended for home decorating.

▪ Where to Find the Perfect Fabric

By now, you probably have a pretty good idea of what you need. Now to find what you want.

Home-Decorating Shops

Stores which specialize in decorator fabrics will also have the linings, trims, hardware, and other accoutrements essential to your plan. More important, the person helping you is likely to be knowledgeable about the stock and about decorating, and can look with a designerly eye at your choices. If you are designing your window treatments but would rather leave the actual construction and/or installation to someone else, such a shop should be able to provide you with names of reliable specialists.

Interior Design Studios

Although they do not usually stock fabrics, they have access to thousands of them. Designers are also able to order out-of-the-ordinary trims, hardware, and other accessories. They can also provide excellent advice on the subject of window treatments.

Mill End and Outlet Stores

Everyone loves bargains, and some great ones can be found in stores which feature mill overruns and end cuts from drapery manufacturers and designers. Be alert when selecting fabric in these places. Many of the bargain fabrics may be seconds, exhibiting flaws you may or may not be able to work around. Soil or stains which landed the piece there in the first place may not disappear with washing or dry cleaning. Check carefully that patterns are not printed off-grain. And if you need (and can find) two separate pieces to make up your required yardage, examine them carefully, in a sunny parking lot if possible, to be sure the color is the same on both.

You may not be able to find out the fiber content of these fabrics, or to obtain the manufacturer's care recommendations. If you fall in love with a mystery fabric, buy two yards, cut the piece in half, and measure each piece precisely. Send one piece to the dry cleaner, and wash and dry the other, then measure them again to check for shrinkage. If the worst happens, you've saved yourself a good bit of money. If the fabric performs well, go back and buy what you need—quickly! Good fabrics don't last long in these stores.

Wallpaper and Paint Stores

The fabrics they sell are made to match wallpapers and are meant to be used for window treatments. Often these stores employ people with decorating experience who can give you counsel. Most of the fabrics must be special ordered.

Fabric Stores

These are the shops that carry fabrics intended for garment-making. You know, by now, what to look for and what to avoid, and you may find fabric that's perfect for your project. Here you can expect guidance in selecting cloth appropriate for your project, helpful sewing tips, and care information.

Estate Sales, Flea Markets, Yard Sales, Antique Shops

It is possible to find some wonderful vintage fabrics—of a quality no longer made or no longer affordable—in draperies and curtains rescued from older homes. A person who is adept at recycling fabric can produce unique window treatments from such treasures. Be careful; the caveats that apply to other fabric bargain sources apply doubly here.

■ Selecting the Decorator Fabric

When you have found a fabric or fabrics you like, there are a few points you should check before you buy.

Patterned fabrics and grain of fabric. A pattern can be woven (or knitted) into the fabric, or it can be printed onto the surface. The process of printing a pattern onto the fabric often causes the cloth to go slightly askew, resulting in a pattern that is printed off grain—not even with the grainlines of the fabric.

The off-grain printing problem is most obvious with horizontal stripes, plaids, or checks. If you like these patterns it is best to look for woven renditions of them rather than printed versions. How to tell the difference? Look at the wrong side of the fabric—a woven pattern will be as obvious on the wrong side as on the right.

Many printed floral patterns and the like will also exhibit a horizontal or vertical design line, which will necessitate matching at any seams and across both panels. Such lines may not be apparent in a small piece of fabric or at close range, but become obvious when a substantial length of the fabric is viewed from a distance. These lines should be straight with the grain of the fabric. With a very stable fabric, one which has no stretch along the lengthwise grain and very little across, an off-grain pattern can be accommodated (see page 53). Decorator fabrics usually are quite stable. Soft, unstable fabric with a pattern that is printed seriously off grain should be avoided like poison ivy.

Width. Does the width of the fabric permit panels to be cut to the size you need without a great deal of waste or a great deal of piecing? If the treatment is to be lined, is lining fabric available in the same width?

Suitability. Check that the fabric has the qualities necessary for the window treatment you plan, such as hand, opacity, stability, wrinkle resistance, and density. Are the care requirements appropriate to its purpose? Does it have the finish treatment you require for stain repellency, mildew resistance, fade-proofing, and so forth? If you are shopping in a store which specializes in decorator fabric, by all means discuss your project with the person helping you—the advice is free, and probably good.

Quantity. Does the store have adequate yardage for your project? If your yardage requirement is great it may not be possible to get it all from a single bolt. There may be subtle color differences between two bolts of the same fabric, so check them very carefully, outside, in natural light. What may seem a slight

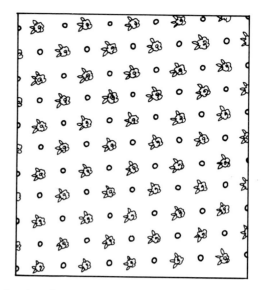

A printed pattern should follow the grain of the fabric, but often does not. Very stable fabric can be cut according to the pattern rather than along the grainline and still retain its shape.

color difference in the store can be jarring when there is one panel of each in a floor-length drapery at home. Once you are aware of a color difference, it is not usually difficult to work around it, perhaps by using the two "colors" at opposite ends of the room.

Before you invest in the large quantity of fabric a window treatment requires, buy two yards of the fabric to take home and test. It is all well and good to look at the fabric in the store and match it to swatches of this and that from your handbag, but you want to subject the fabric to more rigorous testing at home. If it proves to be a bit short of the mark, it should at least be close enough that your purchase will fit into your decorating scheme somehow. And if it is indeed the perfect fabric, you will already have a piece large enough to use for an element of the window treatment, or for an accent in the same room. If you plan to use a coordinating print or solid color, or decorative trims, buy small amounts of those to look at with the main fabric.

Hang the sample in front of the appropriate window along with its lining and interlining. Look at it as objectively as you can while you consider the following checklist.

Color and pattern. Does the fabric blend well with the other elements in the room? Does the pattern work with others in the room? Is the size of the print right for the scale of the room?

Texture. Is the surface finish compatible with the overall feel of the room? A lot of nubby fabric can look too "down home" for a formal room, while the shine of two or three satin-draped windows might overpower a room featuring matte-textured neutral colors.

Suitability. Will the fabric work well for the treatment you are planning? With its lining, will it block out light? Or admit sufficient light? In the quantity that's required, will the weight of the fabric be a problem? Does it drape as required? Will the pattern and its repeat size work with your design?

Washability. If you plan to wash the curtains, you will want to preshrink the fabric; washing the sample will tell you whether you need to allow for shrinkage when you buy the fabric. Measure your sample precisely, then wash, dry, and press it as you intend to do with the finished product. Re-measure to check for

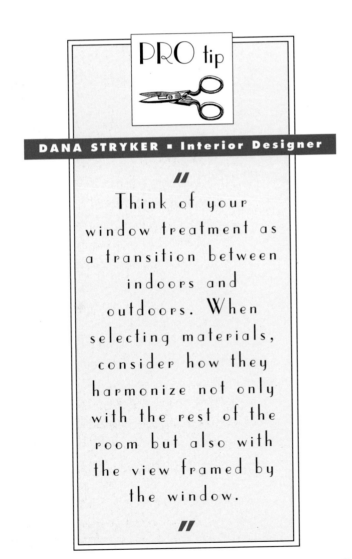

PRO tip

DANA STRYKER ▪ Interior Designer

" Think of your window treatment as a transition between indoors and outdoors. When selecting materials, consider how they harmonize not only with the rest of the room but also with the view framed by the window. "

Top right: The handsome green trim and lining on the swag and jabots echo the foliage outside. The success of the design lies in its prefect proportions and the careful placement of pattern motifs across the swag. The lining and trim of the swag, as well as the face fabric, are cut on the bias to achieve the beautiful drape. **Design: Dianne Ingle**

Bottom right: Gentle pinks and whites are perfect above a baby's crib. Christmas balls, some pink and some clear acrylic, are tied to narrow white ribbons cut to various lengths, with bows of multicolored ribbon adding a festive touch. The ribbon hangers are simply taped securely to the ceiling. A softly shirred valance softens the lines of the functional, light-controlling mini blinds. **Design: Donna Williams**

Bottom far right: No sewing is required to create this exuberant decor for a child's room. The bright colors painted on the window frame are echoed in the purchased bedspread. Grosgrain ribbons in vibrant colors are thumbtacked to each side of the window, and bright plastic blocks are glued across the top, for a room as playful as the small child who lives there. **Design: Donna Williams**

shrinkage. If your window treatment will be dry cleaned it probably is not necessary to send your sample to the cleaner at this point unless the fabric is of suspicious or unknown origin.

If the sample measures up to all these criteria, and is within your budget as well, ask yourself one last question: Will you enjoy living with this fabric for a long, long, long, LONG time?

Once you've decided the fabric is right, make your purchase as soon as you can. A store cannot always reorder an in-stock fabric. Re-check your measurements. Be absolutely sure you are allowing enough extra fabric for the necessary pattern matching. It is always a good idea to buy extra fabric.

Examine the piece carefully as it is unrolled, watching for flaws and for evenness of color printing on patterned fabrics. It is possible to work around minor flaws, and every piece of fabric will have them, but spots, printing glitches, or large slubs (thick pieces of thread in the weaving) have a way of ending up dead center of the finished project just at eye level. If you notice a serious flaw before the fabric is cut, you may be able to negotiate with the store; if you return with the cut fabric after a week or two, you may not. Worse, it might not then be possible to buy additional yardage.

■ Linings and Interlinings

Unless they are designed specifically to admit light, draperies, long curtains, swags and jabots, and valances should always be lined. No other element of a window treatment will contribute as much toward a professional-looking finished project. Lining serves a number of functions. It backs up the face fabric, making it look richer and giving it stability. It covers construction details. It protects the decorator fabric from sun-fading. It increases opacity. It insulates. And if similar linings are used for all window treatments in the home, it gives the house a neat and uniform appearance from outside.

Just as you did when you designed your window

treatment, determine the function your lining has to perform; you should have no trouble finding a lining fabric which exactly fills the bill.

Lining fabrics are available in stores which sell decorator fabrics. Since these linings are manufactured specifically for use in window treatments, they have built-in qualities which make them the best choice for that purpose. They are often sateens, cotton, cotton and polyester, or cotton and rayon and are white or off-white in color. Many are treated with special finishes. Most are preshrunk for dry cleaning; some are washable. They are available in the same range of widths as are decorator fabrics.

Specialized linings. Lining fabrics are manufactured or treated to give them specific qualities. A lining can be made water repellent, crease resistant, flame retardant, or mildew resistant. It can protect against water spotting. There are thermal linings for added insulation, completely opaque blackout linings, and linings designed to reflect the sun away from the window.

Alternative linings. There may be cases where traditional lining fabric will not quite suit your window treatment design. Perhaps your design calls for a strictly decorative lining, as on tails or jabots where you want a coordinating color or print. Or perhaps you are planning a sheer Austrian shade, and your chosen fabric is a little too limp to hold the pouffy quality you would like. A sheer cotton/polyester batiste might provide the necessary body to the fabric without detracting from the light, airy appearance of the shade. Or maybe you are decorating windows which look onto a porch, and you would like a treatment that will blend with the decorating schemes of both the indoor and the outdoor "rooms." A drapery lining which coordinates with the porch chair cushions would create a dual-purpose window treatment.

Many fabrics are perfectly suitable for linings; the advantage of using those made specifically for the purpose is that they eliminate the need for guesswork. If another kind of fabric is to be used, it must be compatible with the face fabric in several ways. It should have the same hand and the same, or lighter, weight. It should have the same amount of lengthwise stretch. It should require the same kind of care. If the face fabric is to be preshrunk so that the window treatment will be washable, the lining must be preshrunk in the same manner.

Remember, too, that such fabrics will not have the special finishes of standard linings.

Interlining. An extra fabric layer placed between the face fabric and lining fabric serves two purposes: It increases the insulative quality of the window treatment and it lends additional body to the face fabric. Thermal interlining fabrics, available where linings are sold, fulfill both functions. If the thermal quality is not needed, a lightweight cotton or cotton blend can be used to enhance the face fabric, and will be less expensive than thermal fabric. Interlining fabric, like lining fabric, should be chosen for compatibility with the face fabric, and must work with the lining as well.

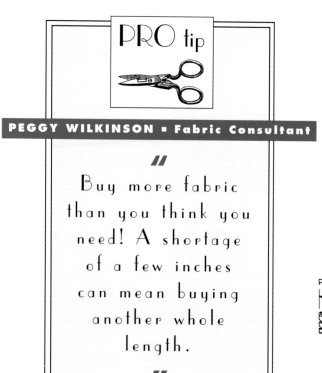

PRO tip

PEGGY WILKINSON ▪ Fabric Consultant

" Buy more fabric than you think you need! A shortage of a few inches can mean buying another whole length. "

▪ Other Materials

Draperies will require some sort of heading stiffener or tape, discussed in the instructions for the specific window treatment styles. You will also need hooks, one for each pleat and one at each end of each panel.

Roman, Austrian, and balloon shades use ring tape, rings, or shirring tape. These materials are described in the instructions for each shade style.

▪ Hardware ▪

Rods and brackets provide support for draperies or curtains and for top treatments. There are hundreds and hundreds of drapery hardware components, and probably as many possible combinations as there are ideas for window treatments. Many of the rods and brackets are made for show as well as for support, and can be made part of the overall design for your window treatments.

There is hardware available to cope with every imaginable shape, size, and oddity a window can offer. There are curved rods for bow windows, shaped rods for bay windows, and swing rods to accommodate small dormer windows. There are hardware accessories to perform every conceivable function—including that of opening and closing draperies by remote control! Special rods and accessories can be ordered through shops which sell drapery fabric.

The quality of the hardware you buy affects both performance and appearance. Better rods are made

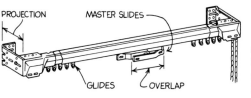

A traverse rod enables draperies to be drawn open or closed easily with cords.

A decorative rod enhances the drapery design.

of heavier metal, capable of supporting even the weightiest draperies without sagging. They also have a durable finish to protect them against corrosion.

Below are descriptions of the basic types of rods and other hardware to give you a starting place as you design your window treatment.

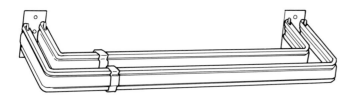

A double curtain rod supports both a valance and curtains, or sheers with heavier outer curtains.

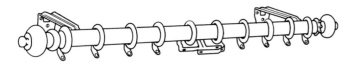

This decorative rod functions like a traverse rod. Eyes below the rings hold the drapery hooks.

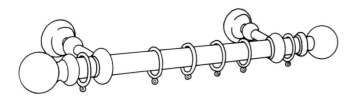

With this rod rings are sewed to the top of the curtain.

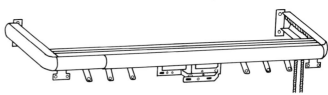

This traverse rod has a decorative finish. The top of the drapery just reaches the bottom of the rod.

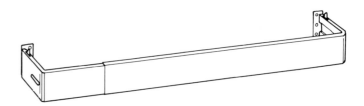

The cornice, or valance, rod is attractive either with a valance or for rod pocket curtains. It is available 2-1/2" or 4-1/2" in depth.

▪ C u r t a i n R o d s

The plain rods are used with curtains with casings, or rod pockets, and for stationary window treatments. Curtain rods are available with clearances ranging from 2" to 5".

Double rods allow for a valance to be hung with the curtains. These have a 1" clearance between the two rods.

Sash rods have approximately 1/4" clearance and most often are used in pairs—one at the top and one at the bottom—with shirred sheer curtains on doors or French windows, for example.

Spring tension rods are plastic-tipped rods which fit snugly inside the window frame against both side jambs; they require no mounting hardware.

Cornice rods, known by the trade names Continental or Dauphine, are plain curtain rods, 2-1/2" or 4-1/2" in depth, which make a decorative feature of the curtain's rod pocket.

Above: In an effective use of hardware, the large rod is covered with the same fabric that lines the panels. Design: Dianne Ingle

Right: The jungle print of the valance echoes the tangle of foliage outside. Tabs, trimmed to match the jabot lining, hang from the top to cover the shirring lines. Design: Kathryn Long

■ Traverse Rods

These rods enable draperies to be opened and closed with a cord. The drapery hooks attach to slides fitted into the rod, and the drapery covers the rod when closed. Traverse rods are available with two-way draw, meaning the draperies open from the center toward each side; or one-way draw, where

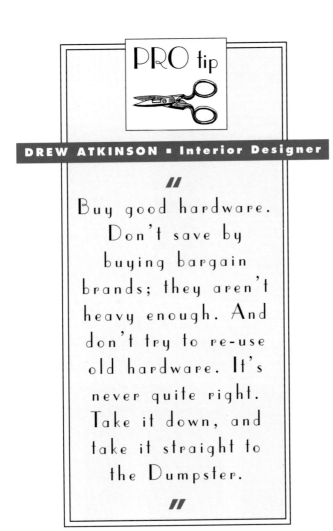

PRO tip

DREW ATKINSON ■ Interior Designer

"Buy good hardware. Don't save by buying bargain brands; they aren't heavy enough. And don't try to re-use old hardware. It's never quite right. Take it down, and take it straight to the Dumpster."

Decorative traverse rods that resemble heavy cafe rods, with matching rings to which the drapery hooks, eliminate the need for a top treatment. They are available with a brass finish, in wood, or painted metal.

Ringless decorative traverse rods carry the drapery slightly lower than do standard traverse rods, so that the rod is visible when the drapery is closed. The slides are concealed at the back of the rod.

Track rods are ceiling mounted and can be shaped to order. The drapery is affixed to carriers which slide along the track on the underside of the rod. Draperies are opened and closed with baton pulls attached at the leading edges rather than with cords.

■ Cafe Rods and Poles

These rods are available in different diameters and are used with rings which either clip or are sewn to the top of the curtain. Most café rods are decorative and may be metal or wood, painted or clear finished, with matching rings and mounting brackets available in some cases.

Elegant top treatments can be achieved by the use of special hardware designed for that purpose. Ornamental swag holders convert a length of plain fabric to a graceful heading. With the tulip-style swag holders you can create intricate rosettes, knots, and poufs without sewing a stitch. Scarf rings and holders inspire artful arrangements using just a few yards of sheer fabric.

Look at hardware options while your project is still in the design stage. You may find some entirely new possibilities to consider.

they open to either the right or left side. They can be mounted on the wall or on the ceiling.

A **double rod** may consist of two traverse rods, or it may be an outer traverse rod with an inner plain rod.

Basic

Techniques

In this section are the terms, the tools, and the techniques essential for the construction of professional-looking window treatments. The procedures described here apply to all window treatment styles. If you are an inexperienced sewer, it would be a good idea, before you start your project, to read through the procedures that apply to the treatment you are making.

■ Basic Terms ■

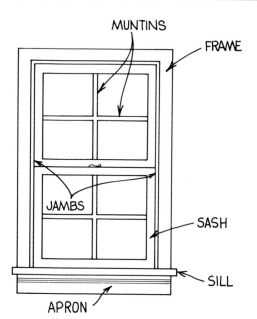

■ Words for Windows

Apron. On a window, the decorative trim below the sill.

Frame. The trim surrounding a window.

Jamb. The inner side and top sections of a window frame.

Muntins. The vertical and horizontal wooden strips which separate panes of glass in a window.

Sill. The lower horizontal part of the window frame, a shelf-like projection.

■ Window Treatment Styles

Austrian shade. A shirred shade constructed with vertical tapes to which rings are attached. Cords threaded through the rings raise and lower the shade.

Balloon shade. Similar to an Austrian shade, but with additional shirring between the tapes, which gives a fuller look when the shade is lowered.

Cornice. A solidly constructed treatment attached above the window to cover the shade or curtain top and rod.

Curtain. A stationary or hand-drawn window treatment, usually unlined, used with rings or having a casing at the top through which a rod is inserted.

Drapery. A window treatment, usually lined and with a pleated heading, which is opened and closed by a cord or track system.

Hourglass curtain. A curtain stretched between two sash rods then tied at the center to give it that shape.

Jabot. Short, stationary side panels used in conjunction with a swag, often with bias-cut lower edges and pleated to show a contrast lining.

Roman shade. A fabric shade which is raised and lowered by cords threaded through rings sewn in vertical rows to the back of the shade. A Roman shade is not shirred, and forms horizontal pleats when it is drawn open.

A softly shirred valance and tails call attention to the spectacular bay window in this elegant master bath. Contrasting trim on the window treatment echoes the painted trim of the cabinets. The graceful curves of the jabots counter the straight lines of the mini blinds behind them. The length of the valance and jabots are perfectly suited to the large proportions of the room. Design: Kathryn Long

41

■ Window Treatment Anatomy

Conventional roll. The situation in which a roller shade is hung with the roller to the inside and the fabric of the shade close to the glass.

Face fabric. This refers to the decorative, outer fabric as opposed to lining or interfacing.

Heading. On a curtain, the extension above the rod casing. On a drapery, the stiffened upper edge which is pleated and to which hooks are attached.

Leading edge. The edge of a drapery panel which moves when the curtain is opened or closed.

Overlap. The distance by which the leading edge of one drapery panel extends over the other at the center.

Panel. A finished section of a drapery or curtain, which may be a single width of fabric, or two or more widths seamed together.

Pattern repeat. With patterned fabric, the vertical or horizontal space occupied by one complete design motif.

Pelmet. A British term for a cornice, or a valance attached to a supporting board.

Return. The end section of a drapery panel which corresponds to the rod projection.

Reverse roll. The situation in which a roller shade is hung with the roller to the outside and the fabric of the shade slightly away from the glass.

Rod pocket. The casing at the top or bottom of a curtain through which the rod is inserted.

Slat pocket. The casing at the lower edge of a window shade through which a wooden slat is inserted to stabilize the edge.

Stackback. The amount of space occupied by draperies when they are fully open. The space occupied by an open shade is usually called *vertical stack*.

Sash curtain. A stationary rod-pocket curtain, usually sheer and usually with both top and bottom rods, which fits closely to the glass of a window or door.

Scarf. An unconstructed top treatment in which a length of fabric is draped or tied over a rod or brackets.

Swag. A top treatment which is softly shaped with horizontal pleats and folds.

Tails. The vertical extensions of a swag which hang at its outer edges.

Tieback. A decorative cord or fabric piece used to hold an opened drapery panel away from the window.

Valance. A top treatment, usually constructed like a short curtain, which conceals the top of a drapery or curtain and its rod.

Once you have made a decision as to style, measure the windows. Make photocopies of the window illustration, and write in the numbers from your windows. If the illustration doesn't look like your window, draw a diagram to use. Careful measurements will ensure that your beautiful new window treatment fits perfectly. Check your measurements, check your measurements.

Don't assume all windows in the room are the same size even if they appear to be. Don't assume the top of a frame is the same distance from the ceiling at one side as it is at the other. Where measurements are concerned, don't assume anything.

Measure with a folding ruler, the carpenter's variety. It is inflexible and will give you more accurate measurements over large areas. Take the measurement diagrams with you when you shop for fabric. You'll be able to tell quickly whether your fabric choice will work with your design, and to get an approximate idea of the yardage you will need.

▪ Calculating Width

What you'll need to know

Use these figures with the Width Requirements chart to figure fabric requirements.

▪Finished width, determined by the total rod length, including projections and overlaps.

▪What is the fullness factor for your fabric? (Fullness factor is the amount of your fabric needed for a rich-looking

finished curtain or drapery.) Refer to the instructions for your treatment style; they may specify a different means of figuring width requirement. For pleated draperies and rod-pocket curtains, use the figures below. If you are using sheer fabric, use 2-1/2 to 3 times the finished width. For medium-weight fabric, use approximately 2-1/2 times the finished width.

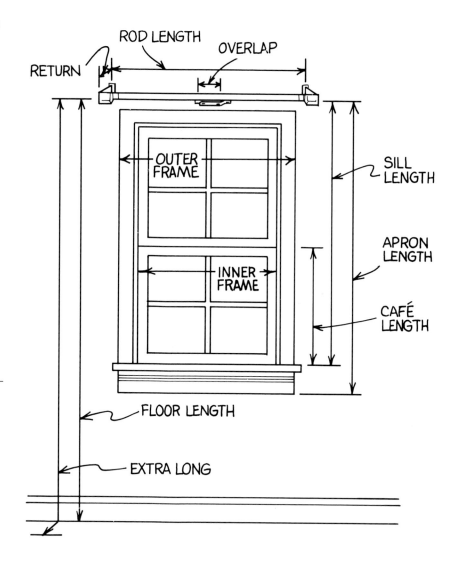

43

Through the use of clean, simple lines and solid colors, this treatment creates a perfect frame for the spectacular scene beyond. Carefully chosen colors include the view in the room's decor. Soft curves of the swag provide contrast to the vertical lines of the draperies and window.
Design: Pam Long

For heavy fabric, use 2 times the width. If your fabric has a large design motif, using slightly less fabric in the width will allow the pattern more prominence.

- To figure side hem allowances, see page 58.
- If you need more than one fabric width to make up your panel width, add 1" for each seam.

Fabric weight or type	Fullness factor (Multiples of fabric width needed for effect)
Light	3–3-1/2
Medium	2–3
Heavy	2–2-1/2

▪ Calculating Length

What you'll need to know

Use these figures with the Length Requirements chart to figure fabric requirements.

- Finished length. The top point from which length is measured depends on the kind of rod you are using; read the measuring instructions for your treatment style for specific information. For floor-length draperies, measure to a point 1/2 to 1" above the floor. For extra-long draperies, add

Width Requirements

Finished width of draperies	_____
Divided by number of panels on rod _____ ÷ _____	_____
Multiply by fullness factor _____ × _____	
Add side hems	+ _____
Add seam allowances	+ _____
Total width per panel	_____

Width of fabric	_____
Number of fabric widths needed per panel (total width ÷ panel width)	_____
Round to next higher half-width	_____

to the floor-length measurement.

- Top hem allowance. Find this in the specific instructions for your window treatment style.
- Bottom hem allowance. See pages 58 and 61.
- If your pattern requires matching (see page 31), what is the vertical repeat? Allow one pattern repeat for each width you require, per panel, beyond the first width. For example, if you need three widths per panel, allow for two additional pattern repeats per panel in your length calculations. Round up to the next whole number.

Length Requirements

For fabrics which do not require pattern matching:	
Finished length	_____
Add bottom hem	+ _____
Add heading or casing	+ _____
Add for minor length adjustments	+ 2"
Total length per panel	_____

For fabrics which require pattern matching:	
Total length per panel (from above)	_____
Vertical pattern repeat (in inches)	_____
▪ Number of repeats needed (round to next higher number)	_____
+ allowance for panels requiring more than one width of fabric.	_____
Total length per panel	_____

▪ Calculating Yardage

Multiply your total length, from the Length Requirements chart, by your total number of widths, from the Width Requirements chart. The result is your yardage requirement. If your fabric will need considerable straightening across the grain, or if it has a printed pattern which is badly off-grain, add several inches per length to the total.

▪ How Much Lining and Interlining?

Whenever possible, lining and interlining materials should be purchased at the same width as the face fabric. If this is not possible, add 1" for seam allowance for each seam needed in the panel.

Lining yardage requirements for draperies and curtains are based on finished length. Add 1" at the top for evening up, and add 3" at the bottom for a 2" doubled hem which will finish 1" above the drapery hemline. For width, add 1" at each side for 2" doubled hems, giving a finished lining 1" narrower at each side than the drapery panel. Read through the specific instructions for the drapery style you plan to make; some styles involve different measurements for lining.

Interlining fabric should be cut to the finished measurements at the sides and bottom. Add 1" at the top to allow for evening the edge.

▪ Installing Curtain and Drapery Rods ▪

As soon as you have determined which you will make, choose and purchase the hardware—rods, brackets, rings, and any other accessories. You will need to know the length of the rod in order to figure fabric width requirements. With long curtains and draperies especially, rods should be installed before measuring for length. And you'll need the length measurement to buy your fabric with accuracy.

Finding the best position for a drapery or curtain rod and attaching it at that point can be frustrating chores. They are best done as team activities, especially with wide rods and traverse rods. It is a good idea to test the rod placement before any holes are drilled, by taping up a sheet or two and studying the effect.

A curtain rod for full-length curtains is usually mounted near the top of the window frame, close to the outer edges. The upper edge of the frame should not be visible above the curtain heading. For curtains covering just the lower half of the window, the rod usually is placed at the midpoint of the window, where the sashes meet. Rods for sash curtains are attached to the door or window just above and just below the glass area.

Traverse rods and other rods used with draw draperies have to be wide enough to allow for stackback (see page 80) and so are mounted outside the window frame.

PRO tip

DREW ATKINSON ▪ Interior Designer

" Measure each window. There's no such thing as a standard window. "

Above: A cathedral window can pose a design problem, solved beautifully here with draw draperies and a well-proportioned swag over just the lower section. The painted center window support continues the theme of the drapery trim. Design: Drew Atkinson

Left: Above these elegant draperies is a magnificent valance, softly fluted in perfect accordance with the printed motifs of the fabric and lined in a small rose check. Design: Kathryn Long

A rod must be level in order for the draperies or curtains to hang straight. But level with what? The use of a carpenter's level is the only way to be sure of a level rod. Rarely is any element of a room's structure really level. A top treatment is good for hiding a situation where rod, window frame, and ceiling represent three different interpretations of "level."

Hardware, especially for long, heavy draperies must be securely attached. Although screws are packaged with the rods, longer ones may hold better. Plastic screw anchors should be used to mount rods on masonry or plaster walls, and toggle bolts or hollow wall anchors on drywall.

Comprehensive mounting instructions are packaged with each rod. More information about the hardware installation for specific window treatment styles is included with the instructions for the treatment.

The guidelines at right apply to the installation of hardware for many different window treatment styles.

- Don't make assumptions about measurements. Measure separately for each rod in the room, even if all windows appear to be the same.
- It takes two people to determine the best location for the rod, and it takes two people to put it there. With traverse rods, particularly, it's nice if one of them has some experience with this kind of thing.
- Before permanently affixing the rod, note its appearance from *outside* the window.
- Coordinate the placement of the top treatment with the rod placement, allowing for any necessary clearance between the two.

There are people who install window treatments for a living, usually working in conjunction with interior designers. If you are overwhelmed by the prospect of installing a complicated treatment, ask a local designer to refer you to a professional installer.

The Workroom and Equipment

A well-equipped, well-lighted place to work makes any project more enjoyable—and perhaps more successful. In this section are tips for setting up a work area, along with suggestions for tools and accessories to simplify drapery-making tasks.

■ Table Space

You will need a flat surface, the larger the better, to straighten, pin, and cut fabric. Consider renting one or two long folding tables for the duration of your project, or buying an inexpensive one. A door or sheet of plywood placed across sawhorses makes a fine temporary table. Cinderblocks under the legs of the sawhorses will raise the table to a workable height.

PRO tip

GINGER KINZEL ■ Interior Designer

"
It is essential to have a proper work table. You must lay the fabric flat to square it.
"

If your project is long draperies, pressing also will be easier on a table. (Don't use the dining room table for pressing—steam can damage the finish and warp the wood.) For pressing, pad the table. Place on the table several layers of old wool or cotton blankets, or cotton (not polyester) batting, folded to fit the tabletop. Cover them with an old sheet or piece of inexpensive muslin 6" or 8" larger all around than the table. Fold the muslin to the underside of the table, pull it taut, and tack or staple it, beginning with the center of each side, then the corners, then between the original tacks, and so forth.

■ S e w i n g   M a c h i n e

For making window treatments, it is essential that your machine produce a good straight stitch and that the thread tension be adjusted correctly. It should be powerful enough, and the feed mechanism effective enough, to sew evenly through several layers of heavy fabric. Before you start your project, check that the bobbin and the space under the feed dog teeth are free of lint. If your machine requires it, oil according to the instruction manual.

Sewing machine needles. Change the needle each time you begin a new project. A dull or damaged needle will produce unsightly stitching and can damage your fabric. Sewing heavily treated fabric will dull a needle quickly; it will probably need to be changed again mid-project. Tightly woven synthetic fabrics can also shorten the life of a needle.

Always use the needle *type* called for in your machine instruction manual; different needles are made for different machines and there is no generic. The size needle you use will depend upon your fabric. For sheers, size 80/12 should work; for heavily finished cottons or linens, a 90/14 or even 100/16 may be needed.

Standard machine needles have a slightly rounded, or "universal," point. With very tightly woven or heavily finished fabric, this needle can cause a popping sound as it penetrates the fabric, and skipped stitches may result. If this happens, try to locate *sharp* needles, which are often packaged as "jeans" needles. They are available in standard sizes.

Sewing machine accessories. Certain projects or techniques can be accomplished faster, more easily, and more accurately with the use of specialized presser feet or other machine accessories. With the amount of sewing involved in a window treatment, this might be a good time to invest in additional accessories. A **ruffler attachment**, for example, can save a tremendous amount of time and aggravation if you are adding ruffles to curtains. A **walking foot** or **even-feed foot** is valuable in eliminating uneven seams in loosely woven fabrics, and in matching plaids or prints. Others, like the **blind hemmer**, **zipper foot**, and **overlock foot**, may have come with your machine but you might not use them frequently enough to feel comfortable with them. Dust them off now and practice a bit; they can both save time and improve the quality of your workmanship if you will let them.

■ S e r g e r

Your serger deserves the same pre-project cleaning, oiling, and needle change as your sewing machine. Be sure the tension is balanced, and that the knife blades are sharp and free of nicks.

If you have been putting off buying a serger, a window treatment project is exactly the excuse you have been waiting for: It can cut your sewing time in half. The serger stitches, trims, and overcasts a seam all in one operation, and it is fast. Its stitch formation process is different from that of a sewing machine—there is no bobbin—and it handles tricky fabrics more easily than a sewing machine does.

■ C u t t i n g   E q u i p m e n t

Cutting board. One or two of the heavy cardboard kind, printed with a grid, will be helpful for straightening fabric as well as for cutting.

Rotary cutter and mat. This cutting wheel, used with a heavy ruler, is fast and accurate for the long, straight cuts required in making window treatments. A special mat must be used with the cutter to prevent dulling the blade and damaging the cutting table.

Shears. Good 8" or 9" shears with sharp blades are essential. Heavier ones will cut thick fabrics more easily.

Pinking shears. For many fabrics, pinking provides the best seam finish.

Trimming scissors. Handiest is a short, pointed style with fairly wide blades, which will cut through heavy layers of fabric.

■ Measuring and Marking Tools

Steel spring-return tape. Available from hardware stores, this tape measure is longer than most plastic or cloth tapes, and will not stretch.

Carpenter's square or framing square. It is an L-shaped, heavy metal ruler for squaring fabric, and can also be used to cut with a rotary cutter.

Folding rule. This is another carpenter's tool. It is rigid and thus essential for accurate measurements over large areas.

Spring clamps. These are helpful in holding the fabric securely to the table for squaring, pinning, and cutting.

Seam gauge. This short ruler has an adjustable marker and is valuable for measuring hems and seams.

Chalk marker. A plastic container filled with powdered chalk, this tool produces a very fine line.

Water-soluble fabric marking pen. Handiest is the kind which does not contain disappearing ink. The ink usually is easy to remove with a wet finger or damp cloth, but can react strangely with certain dyes. Test it on each different fabric.

Calculator. Making window treatments requires a good bit of arithmetic.

■ Sewing Accessories and Notions

Pins. Several different kinds will be useful. Glass-headed pins are very sharp and easy to see in the fabric, and the heads won't melt when touched with a hot iron. T-pins are stronger, and useful for pinning fabric to the cutting board to straighten it. Quilting pins have plastic heads and are longer and heavier than dressmakers' pins.

Hand sewing needles. Assorted sharp needles will serve for most drapery-making needs; heavier needles are better for tacking pleats in headings.

Thimble. If you can use one, it may save your fingertip when you sew by hand through thick pleats.

Seam ripper. Or, more kindly, "seam improver," is the safest way to remove a line of stitching.

Tube turner. Best is the kind which utilizes a heavy-gauge metal tube; a spiral-tipped wire is inserted into it to pull the fabric through.

Liquid fray preventer. Applied to raw edges of fabric, it will help stop raveling. It dries clear and slightly stiff.

Glue. A good-quality white glue is best for many of the non-sewn construction steps.

■ Pressing Equipment

A good **steam iron** is essential for any sewing project. Steam pressing sets the stitching lines and shapes the article. Some fabrics, such as chintz and fabrics containing acetate, are prone to water spotting, so with those it's important that the iron not leak or sputter. A **pressing cloth** should be used with certain fabrics (chintz again) to prevent iron shine or marking along seam and hemlines. A **hand steamer** is convenient for removing wrinkles after the draperies are hung, and for training window treatments after installation.

All fabric should receive some attention before it is cut and sewn. What should be done depends upon the fiber content of the fabric, the manufacturer's finish, and whether it will be washed or dry cleaned after it is made up. A little work at this point can go a long way toward preventing unpleasant surprises later.

Preshrinking the Fabric

Preshrinking simply means subjecting the fabric to the same treatment it will receive as a finished item. If you plan to machine wash and dry your curtains, then do the same with the fabric before you cut. Remember that any other materials which will be used in the curtains—trim, heading tape, lining, or interfacing—must be preshrunk in the same manner as the outer fabric. Then press or iron the fabric(s), working with the lengthwise grain, and taking care not to stretch it out of shape. *Always, always* preshrink fabric that will later be washed.

If your curtains or draperies will be dry-cleaned, you probably should not wash the fabric in advance. Decorator fabrics are often labeled "preshrunk," but may shrink a bit with dry cleaning. If slight shrinkage will be a problem with the design you are planning, you might consider having a dry cleaner preshrink the fabric before you begin.

An alternative precautionary step with dry cleanable fabric is simply to press the fabric with a steam iron, being careful not to stretch it. You can square the grain of the fabric at the same time. This is a good procedure to follow with conventional lining fabrics, too.

Straightening the Grain

This procedure is very important; if you are making long drapery panels, it is absolutely essential. It may take some time to do this, but if it isn't done the draperies will never hang straight. With most fabrics the grain governs the way draperies or curtains will hang. The fabric stretches least along the lengthwise grain, and drapery panels are cut in that direction so they will not sag out of shape after hanging for a time. During the manufacturing or printing process, or when it is rolled on bolts, fabric may go slightly askew. The grain must be squared before the fabric is cut. This procedure is especially important with loosely woven fabrics and those not intended specifically for home decorating use.

Sheer, soft, and lightweight fabrics. The grain can be straightened easily if a crossgrain thread is pulled. Clip through the selvage near the cut end of the fabric, and carefully pull a thread to mark the crosswise grain of the piece. Then, with a carpenter's square or the grid lines of your cutting board, arrange the fabric so that the lengthwise grain is exactly perpendicular to the cross grain.

A new piece of fabric often has the shape indicated by the solid lines above. It must be squared before cutting so that the lengthwise grain is perpendicular to the crosswise grain, as shown by the dotted lines.

Printed patterns. Such a pattern may exhibit a horizontal line which should be, but probably is not, parallel to the cross grain of the fabric. To compensate for this, decorator fabrics are usually heavily finished to give them stability enough that they can be cut off the straight grain without ill effect. Dressmaker fabrics, or any soft or loosely woven fabric with an off-grain printed pattern should not be used for draperies or curtains.

To prepare a printed fabric for cutting, align the selvages with the grid on the cutting board, and make the horizontal cuts with the pattern lines rather than with the cross grain of the fabric.

Woven patterns. Fabrics such as plaids and checks can usually be squared by steam pressing. Fold the piece with the selvages together, align the cut edges precisely along the pattern lines, and pin or baste. Then pat at it with a steam iron, pulling gently, until there are no diagonal wrinkles.

If your fabric doesn't fit into any of these categories, try first the method suggested for woven patterns.

▪ Cutting Your Fabric

If it is necessary to use half widths to make up a panel, plan for the half width to be at the outer edge of the panel. This will mean having a left and a right panel for two-way draw curtains or draperies. Note, too, placement of any pattern and whether it will need to be matched across the fabric as well as vertically.

If the draperies will be dry-cleaned, selvages usually need not be cut away on decorator fabrics, unless they are a different color or are printed with the manufacturer's name and will show through to the right side. Check this by holding the fabric up to the window while the sun is shining. If the selvages are not trimmed off, clip through them at 1" to 3" intervals to prevent them from shrinking and causing puckered seams.

1. Lay out your fabric on the work table or floor so that it is square and flat. Take care to keep the excess

fabric neatly folded or rolled, as best you can, so it doesn't crease. Find the starting point for the lower edge of your first panel. For unpatterned fabrics, use

PRO tip

CAROL PARKS ▪ Author

"
Never cut into a piece of fabric after 9 p.m.
"

the straightened edge as described above.

If your fabric has a large or distinctive motif, particularly one which creates a horizontal line across the width, you want to decide where the pattern should appear on the finished panel. Professional

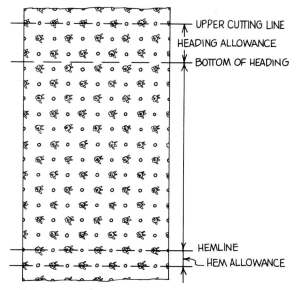

UPPER CUTTING LINE
HEADING ALLOWANCE
BOTTOM OF HEADING

HEMLINE
HEM ALLOWANCE

For fabric with a prominent pattern, determine the best placement for an entire lengthwise pattern repeat, then measure down to the lower edge and up to the top cutting line.

designers use this rule of thumb: On long draperies, a full pattern repeat should appear slightly below the bottom of the heading; for apron-length or sill-length draperies, there should be a complete pattern repeat just above the lower edge. To find the bottom cutting line for your fabric using this guideline, subtract the heading depth plus about 1" from your finished length measurement. Position your ruler at the top of a pattern repeat, and measure that distance down the fabric to find the bottom cutting line for the piece. Then, of course, measure back up the fabric by the full cutting length to find the cutting line for the top of the piece.

If you are working with a one-way design, be sure you are starting at the bottom of the panel.

2. Cut across for the lower edge.

3. Measure, and cut for the top.

4. Place this piece on top of the next section of fabric to use as a guide for cutting the second piece. Be sure all edges are aligned, and that any pattern matches. Pin if necessary before you cut.

5. Cut remaining pieces in the same way, using the original each time as a guide.

If your pattern is ambiguous, or if you are using napped fabric, it is a good idea to mark the top of each piece so that when you assemble them they all will be right side up. Draw a big X on the wrong side, near the top with a fabric marking pen, or mark each piece with a strip of masking tape.

• Construction Techniques •

The construction methods and sewing steps described in this section are used in a number of different window treatments. If you are an experienced sewer, many will be familiar to you. If you are a novice, you should be able to find here all the stitches and procedures you need to complete your project.

• Professional Pressing

For ease in working with large pieces of fabric, pad a table to use for cutting and pressing (see page 49). Before you start your project, clean the gunk from the bottom of your iron, and use an internal iron cleaner—unless the manufacturer forbids it—so you will have the greatest possible steam production.

The extra piece of fabric you bought (you did, didn't you?) can be used to determine the iron temperature and amount of moisture which give the best results with your particular fabric. Test to see whether water will spot the fabric; if so, use a slightly damp pressing cloth with a dry iron. Glazed fabrics, such as chintz, may be sensitive about right-side pressing.

• Press every seam before you sew across it. First press the line of stitching, then press the seam open or to one side.

• Don't slide the iron on the fabric. Press one spot, lift the iron, and press the next spot.

• To remove a stubborn crease, rub lightly with a fairly wet face cloth, then press.

• To prevent the edge of the seam allowance from leaving a visible line on the right side of the fabric, place a strip of brown kraft paper between the seam allowance and the outer fabric while pressing the seam.

• Testing Your Fabric

Every piece of fabric is unique. Each will respond to slightly different sewing and pressing techniques. Use your sample fabric again to determine the stitch length and tension settings that will produce a smooth, pucker-free seam. You will be able to tell whether the seams should be double-stitched, or overcast, or pinked. Also try a line of stitching through several layers of the fabric to see how the same settings will work for hems and headings.

▪ Stitches and Seams

A stitch that works well on one fabric may not be right for another. If the fabric you are using is a new one in your sewing experience, experiment on your fabric sample to see which stitch and what settings are best. A seam which puckers slightly in a 12" sample can be a disaster on floor-length draperies.

▪ For the techniques described in this book 1/2" seam allowance is used unless otherwise noted.

▪ Pin all seams with right sides together, pins perpendicular to the seamline, unless instructed otherwise. Do not sew over pins.

▪ To secure the ends of a seam, backstitch the ends (a few stitches in reverse, then forward again), or sew the first and last 1/2" of the seam with a very short stitch length.

▪ For a pucker-free seam, hold the fabric taut with both hands, behind and in front of the needle, while you sew. Take care not to pull the fabric—let the machine's feed mechanism do the work.

Plain Straight Stitch Seam

This is by far the most commonly used seam for most fabrics and in most situations, and it's the quickest to accomplish.

The stitch length will vary with the fabric; try 8 to 12 stitches to the inch for cotton decorator fabric. If the seam puckers, shorten the stitch length slightly.

With softer fabrics, and for long vertical seams in drapery panels, reinforce or finish the seam by one of the methods described below. With stable fabrics and seams of moderate length, the seam may be pressed open.

Reinforced Plain Seam

This seam is good for loosely woven fabrics and for very heavy curtains or draperies in which the seams will be strained.

Sew as for a plain seam. Sew another line of straight stitching 1/8" away, inside the seam allowance. Press seam allowances to one side.

Self-bound Seam

Raw edges are enclosed, which makes this a good seam for fabrics which ravel and for curtains which will be washed. The double stitching also serves to strengthen the seam. For this seam, trim off wide selvages; clip narrow ones at frequent intervals.

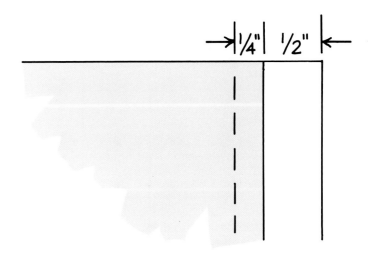

1. With fabrics right sides together and the lower piece extending 1/2" beyond the upper piece, stitch 3/4" from the edge of the lower piece.

Place the fabrics together so that the raw edge of the lower piece extends 1/2" beyond the edge of the upper piece. Sew as for a plain seam, 3/4" from the edge of the lower layer. Fold the wider seam allowance to the narrower so that the raw edges meet. Then fold again, bringing the second fold almost to the stitching line. Press. Stitch again close to the inner fold.

French Seam

This seam also encloses raw edges and works well with sheer fabrics. Selvages should be trimmed off when a French seam is used.

Pin fabrics with *wrong* sides together. Sew a straight seam with slightly less than 1/4" seam

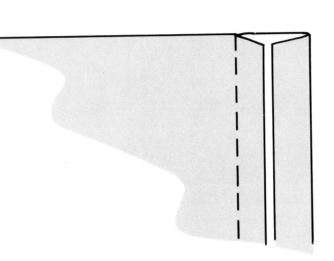

2. Fold the raw edge of the wider seam allowance toward the raw edge of the narrow seam allowance so the raw edges meet. Press.

1. With wrong sides together and raw edges aligned, stitch 1/4" from raw edges. Trim seam allowances to 1/8". Fold seam allowances to one side, press.

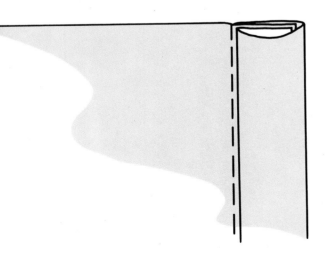

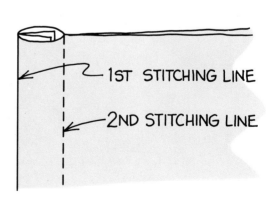

3. Fold the outer folded edge to the stitching line, press, stitch again close to the inner fold.

2. Fold wrong side out along the stitching line; press the fold. Stitch 1/4" from the fold.

allowance. Trim seam allowances to 1/8"; press to one side. Now fold on the stitching line on the wrong side of the fabric, enclosing the raw edges; press. Stitch again 1/4" from the fold.

Seam Finishes

Don't overcast seam allowances unless it's truly necessary; each line of stitching draws up the fabric slightly and can result in puckered seamlines if overdone. Use overcast stitches if the curtains will be washed and the fabric tends to ravel. If the treatment will be dry cleaned, overcasting should be used only if the fabric frays badly.

Most machines have built-in overcasting or zigzag stitches. Experiment with the different stitches and the different length and width settings to find the combination which will produce the neatest results on your particular fabric.

On medium or lightweight fabrics, overcasting can produce a firm ridge at the edge of the seam allowance which can show on the right side after pressing. To avoid this problem, stitch so that on its outward swing the needle penetrates the fabric just a thread short of the raw edge rather than actually oversewing the edge. Or sew the line of overcast stitching about 1/8" from the straight stitch line, then trim the raw edges close to the second line of stitching.

Pinked Seam Allowances

For plain seams which are pressed open, trimming with pinking shears can provide a nice finish and prevent raveling. First stitch along each seam allowance with a straight stitch, about 1/8" from the seamline.

Serger Stitches

Whatever model serger you own, be sure the tension is adjusted to produce a seam that will not pull apart and does not pucker.

Five-thread seams. These strong seams provide good support in long, heavy draperies and with heavy fabrics. With lighter fabrics, be sure the stitch doesn't draw up along the seamline.

Four-thread seams. Four-thread seams can be adjusted to suit almost all fabrics. Keep the left needle tension tight enough that the seam will hold, and the looper tensions loose enough that they don't draw in the edges.

Three-thread seams. A three-thread seam probably will not hold except in short, lightweight curtains. With a three-thread overlock, it would be better to sew seams with a sewing machine straight stitch and overcast, if necessary, with the serger.

A three-thread set-up can produce an excellent seam for sheer curtains. Use the rolled hem setting or attachments. Set the lower looper tension somewhat looser than for a rolled hem, and the stitch length somewhat longer. This stitch will hold well in sheer fabric, and will produce a neatly finished seam.

▪ Vertical Seams: Joining the Widths

If panels require more than one width of fabric, piece the widths together first. A section which is less than a full width of the fabric should be placed at the outer edge of the panel, at the side of the window. Finish the seams, if necessary, and press.

Selvages need not be removed from the edges to be seamed unless they are a different color or are printed with the manufacturer's name and will show through to the right side. Check this against the window, with the sun shining in.

Matching Patterns

Keep in mind that a plaid or print must be matched along the seamline, not at the edges of the fabric. If you are working with a pattern which requires careful matching, a walking foot or even-feed foot is worth its

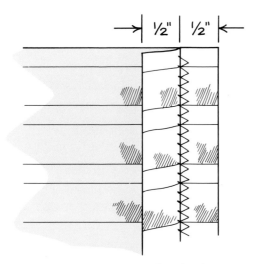

½" ½"

To match patterns accurately, fold back one seam allowance and baste with a zigzag stitch. Loosen the upper thread tension and use a long stitch length.

weight in winning lottery tickets! Be sure to support the fabric behind and in front of the needle as you stitch so there is no pull from either direction; these presser feet do not grip the fabric as tightly as does the regular feed mechanism and uneven stitches can result.

Here is another trick for matching prints and plaids. Place the pieces to be seamed with their right sides together. Fold back the seam allowance of the top piece, so that you are seeing the right side of the fabric on both seam allowances. Pin. Loosen the upper thread tension by about one number and set the machine for a long, medium-width zigzag stitch. Stitch, aligning the fabric so that you catch the folded edge of the fabric by a single thread. Now unfold the folded edge and stitch a plain seam.

■ Hems

Traditionally, the bottom of the panel is hemmed before the sides. If you are not confident of your measurements, or if this is your first window treatment project, or if you suspect your fabric may stretch, you may want to baste the bottom hem and hang the draperies for a week to be sure of the length. In this case, stitch the side hems to within 10" to 12" of the bottom, and finish them after the permanent bottom hem is sewn.

Draperies and curtains traditionally have double hems at sides and lower edges. The size of the hems depends on the weight of the fabric, the depth of the heading, and the length of the curtains. Heavier fabrics need slightly wider hems than lightweight ones. Longer draperies look better with deeper bottom hems, while a narrower hem looks right on a short curtain. The total hem allowance for double-fold side hems should be from 2" to 3", which will give a finished hem of 1" to 2". A bottom hem allowance should be between 3" and 10". The bottom hem should appear proportionate to the total length of the panel: A 1-1/2" finished hem would be perfectly appropriate for short cotton cafe curtains in the kitchen, and a finished hem of 5" for floor-length silk draperies would give them a rich look.

The norm for long draperies is a hem the same width as the heading.

There are three basic hemming techniques. Each is best in certain situations or with certain fabrics, and each method has its devotees.

Measuring and Pressing Hems

Always press and pin the hems before you stitch. A seam gauge is handy for marking hems.

1. On the edge to be hemmed, turn the full hem allowance to the wrong side, and press.

2. Fold in the raw edge almost to the crease; press.

3. Pin, and stitch according to one of the methods below.

Another timesaver is a hem guide made from a piece of unprinted cardboard approximately 12" long.

1. With a waterproof pen, draw a line, parallel with the long edge of the cardboard, the same distance from the edge as the total depth of your hem.

2. Draw a second line for the second fold.

3. Place the cardboard on the fabric and fold the fabric up over it to the inner line, and press.

4. Turn the raw edge in toward the crease, pressing a second fold at the outer line on the cardboard.

5. Pin, and stitch according to one of the methods below.

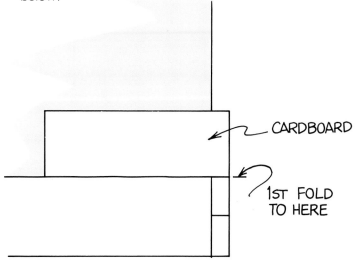

1. Fold the fabric over the cardboard template, aligning the raw edge with the second line.

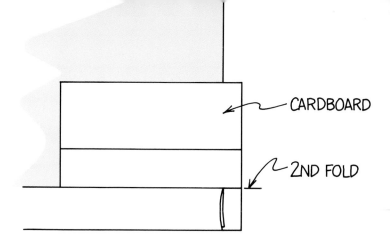

2. Fold the fabric over the template again, aligning the folded edge with the first line on the template.

Machine Blind Hem

With some practice you *can* master your sewing machine's blind hem foot. Pull out the instruction book and try again; the only tricky part is folding the fabric correctly. If this stitch leaves a visible crease at the hemline on the right side, adjust your fabric so that a smaller stitch is taken on the outer fabric, or loosen the upper thread tension slightly. Test first on your sample fabric. Always baste the hem, close to the fold at the lower edge, before stitching.

Machine Straight Stitch Hem

This is a quick and easy hem, and it's perfectly acceptable for casual curtains and for the lower edges of linings. It is not elegant enough for a formal window treatment such as long draperies.

Test the stitch length and tension on your sample. Fold and press the hems as described above. Pin and stitch on the *right* side whenever possible. With most machines, the right side stitching line looks neater. If your machine has no seam guide marking to accommodate stitching this distance from the edge, use the quilting guide or place a strip of masking tape on the base of the machine.

Hand-stitched Blind Hem

Yes, the pros still do this. Put a good movie on the VCR and find a comfortable place to sit where you can spread out the fabric to avoid crumpling it, or work at your table and use clamps to secure the fabric.

Press and pin as described above. Slipstitch the hem with fairly loose stitches, catching just a thread or so of the outer fabric.

Using Weights

Nearly any line of machine stitching will draw up the fabric to some extent. A drapery weight or two placed in the hem at the base of each vertical line of stitching will ease the panel back into shape at these points. A weight just inside the fold of each side hem will help the edges to hang smoothly. Some draperies need weights along the hemline, too. Lightweight curtains can billow in a breeze or draft; weights made especially for sheers can be used along the hemline to keep the curtains in place. Fairly stiff fabrics need to be vertically trained, and hemline weights will pull them down just enough to shape them. Weights can be hand tacked to the inner fold of the hem at 3" to 4" intervals across the lower edge.

Mitered Corners

An attractive and professional look can be achieved by mitering the lower corners of a drapery panel.

1. Measure, fold, press, and pin the side hems. With a machine blind hem or by hand, stitch both side hems to a point about 12" above the lower edge.

2. Measure, fold, press, and pin the bottom hem. Stitch to within 12" of each side.

3. Unfold the hems at one corner. Note that there are two intersections where the side hem folds cross the bottom hem folds.

4. At the *inner* intersection of the fold lines, fold the corner toward the wrong side of the panel at perfect right angles to the bottom and sides, so that the fold is on a 90-degree angle. Press the new fold, taking care not to "erase" the original fold lines.

5. Now re-fold the hems on their original fold lines. The new diagonal fold lines at the corner

should just meet, but not overlap. Trim and clip the inner section of the hem to accomplish this. Check that the corner is still square, then press.

6. Whipstitch the diagonal folds together. Complete the side and bottom hems.

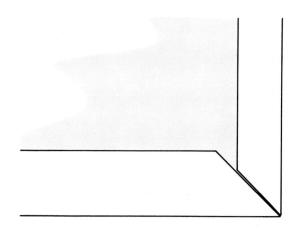

After pressing the mitered corner, hand stitch the diagonal folds together. Don't catch the outer fabric in the stitching.

CURTAINS

Curtains are the most versatile of window treatments. They can be long or short, casual or formal, richly embellished in all sorts of ways or left quite plain. To distinguish them from draperies, curtains are usually stationary on their rod and held back from the window midway down; or they can be hand drawn, like cafe curtains. They may be used in conjunction with draperies to diffuse the light entering a room or for privacy. Above all, curtains can be easy and quick to make!

On the following pages are a number of curtain styles from which to choose. Each one offers all sorts of possibilities for variation, with decorative trims, unusual tiebacks, or imaginative rod treatments. Find a style that suits your purpose, then let your imagination guide you.

· Curtain Rods ·

Before you measure for your curtains and figure your fabric yardage, you need to decide which rod style you will use. Curtain rods fall into two broad categories: flat and round. The flat rods, which usually project from the wall, are available in standard widths or as wider "cornice" rods. Round rods can be functional, meant for use with rod pocket curtains, or they can be a design element in the window treatment. Decorative rods are often intended for use with curtains to which rings are sewn or attached, or with tab top curtains. Or they can be covered with fabric and used with stationary panels. Round rods are supported by brackets which are mounted on the wall. Spring tension rods—round rods which are available in varying diameters—are designed to fit tightly against the side jambs of the window. Sash rods are mounted flush against the window sash or

trim. These are usually used in pairs, in casings at both top and bottom of a curtain.

· Measuring ·

When you have decided upon a curtain style and rod style, refer to page 43 for instructions on measuring and figuring fabric yardage requirements. The specific instructions for making your curtain style may contain additional information which will influence your measurements; read through those, too.

Length can be measured more accurately if the rod is installed first. Determine finished length by measuring from the bottom of the rod to the point at which the curtain will end.

The depth of lower hems on curtains depends upon length and the weight of the fabric. For long curtains in a medium-weight fabric, a 4" double hem is standard, which means adding 8" as the hem allowance. For apron or sill-length curtains, a 3" double hem is suitable to the length. Sheer curtains need proportionately deeper hems to ensure that they hang nicely—4", doubled, for shorter lengths and 5" for long curtains.

Allowance for side hems can be figured at 4" per panel, which gives 1" finished hems.

To measure for the casing—also known as a rod pocket—first measure the diameter of the rod. If the rod is under 1" in diameter, add 1/2" to the diameter measurement for the casing. If the rod diameter is more than 1", allow an additional inch.

If a heading will be used, double the depth of the heading to determine the heading allowance, and add 1/2" seam allowance.

• Patterned Fabrics •

If your fabric has a large design motif and/or a horizontal pattern orientation, consider the placement of the pattern before your fabric is cut. A full pattern repeat usually should be positioned just above the hemline on shorter curtains. On long curtains, place the top of a pattern repeat an inch or two below the rod. See page 53 for instructions on how to cut for pattern placement.

• Before You Begin •

If you plan to wash your curtains, it is essential to preshrink the fabric before you cut. Selvages should be trimmed from fabrics which will be washed, or clipped at 1" intervals. It is also important to straighten the grain so the curtains will hang nicely. See pages 52 and 53 for detailed instructions on fabric preparation and cutting.

Read the information about choosing and testing stitches (page 54), and the detailed instructions for hemming (page 58) before you begin to sew. Those sections contain information on techniques which are used in all the curtain-making projects.

•Rod Pocket Curtains•

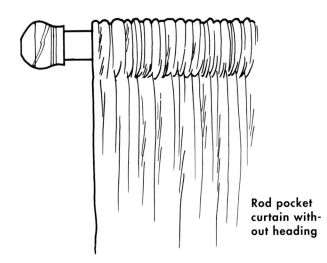

Rod pocket curtain without heading

Fast and easy to make, rod pocket curtains require only hems and a simple casing, and they are ready to hang.

1. Prepare and cut the fabrics as described above.

2. Join vertical seams if necessary.

3. Stitch the bottom hem, then the side hems, referring to the detailed instructions on page 58.

4. Along the top edge, fold 1/2" to the wrong side; press.

5. Fold this edge again to the wrong side by half the casing allowance measurement.

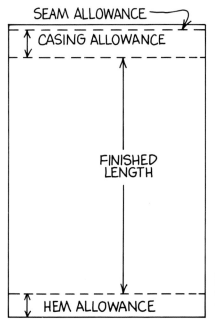

Fabric layout, rod pocket curtain without heading

6. Pin close to the fold for several inches. Slip the pinned section of the casing over the rod to make sure there is enough ease.

7. Re-pin, placing pins perpendicular to the edge, and stitch close to the fold. Press all stitching lines.

• Rod Pocket Curtain with Heading

A ruffled heading above the rod adds a decorative finish to a simple rod pocket curtain. A soft or lightweight fabric may not have enough body to support a deep heading, leaving the heading to droop over

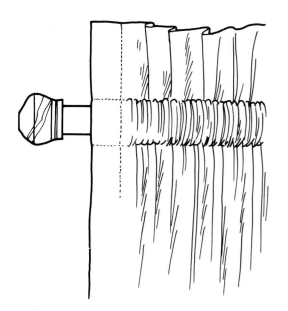

Rod pocket curtain with heading

the rod. If your design sounds like just such a combination, interface the heading as described in Step 4 of the instructions.

1. Read the Before You Begin section, above.

2. Complete Steps 1 through 4 of the instructions for the plain rod pocket curtain, above.

3. Fold the upper edge again to the wrong side to form a hem equal to half the combined casing and heading allowances.

4. If you need to interface the heading, cut a strip of lightweight fusible interfacing the depth of the heading and slightly less than the width of the panel. Open up the fold of the heading. Place a long edge of the interfacing against the fold line at the top of the back side of the heading, on the wrong side of the fabric. Fuse according to the manufacturer's instructions. Re-fold along the top; press.

5. Mark the heading depth with a chalk line. Pin along the lower fold line.

6. Stitch across the curtain close to the fold line, and again along the chalk line.

▪ Lined Rod Pocket Curtains

Lined curtains look neater from outside the window, and lining adds body and fullness to the curtain. Curtain lining can be made according to either of

the methods for lining draperies, page 89, but there is a quicker method which works well with shorter curtains of light to medium weight fabric.

Following the instructions for the plain rod pocket curtain, determine finished width and length of the curtain, and determine the allowance for the casing, and for the heading if you plan to add one. Width also is figured as for the rod pocket curtain.

For the cut length, add 1/2" seam allowance to the casing and heading allowances at the top. At the bottom, add the desired width of the finished hem (this hem will not be doubled) and add 1/2" seam allowance.

For width, add 2" at each side for doubled 1" side hems. If finished width requires more than one width of fabric, add 1" for each seam.

For the lining, measure from the bottom of the rod to the desired length. *Subtract* the finished hem allowance, and add 1/2" at top and at the bottom for seam allowances.

1. Stitch vertical seams, if necessary.

2. With right sides together and raw edges aligned, sew the face fabric to the lining across the top and across the bottom. You will have a tube shape.

3. Press and stitch the side hems in both curtain and lining.

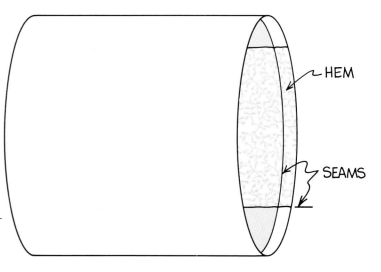

HEM

SEAMS

Lined rod pocket curtain, Step 3

4. Using the original measurements, fold the piece to allow for the casing (and heading) at the top and the hem at the bottom. Press.

5. Stitch across the top to form the casing.

6. At the bottom, hand-stitch the two layers together at each side from the lower edge to the seamline at the top of the hem.

▪ Ruffled Curtains ▪

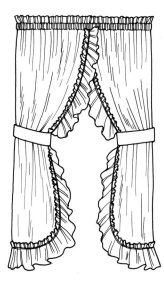

For this unlined curtain, both edges of the ruffle are finished. It is then gathered and sewed onto the right side of the curtain.

Always popular, ruffled curtains create a comfortable, warm atmosphere in any room. With these curtains, ruffles are sewn onto the right side, along the leading edges and at the bottom. A ruffler attachment and a narrow hemmer presser foot make short work of the project.

For these curtains, add 2" to the finished dimensions for hem allowance at the outer edges. At the leading and lower edges add 1/2". Add for a plain rod pocket at the top.

Ruffles can be made of the curtain fabric, or in a coordinating fabric of the same or lighter weight. For each ruffle, allow 2-1/2 times the finished measurement of the leading and lower edges for a medium-weight fabric; 3 times the measurement in a lightweight fabric. Cut fabric strips to total this measurement. For long curtains, cut the strips 4-1/2" wide; for short curtains, 4" wide.

1. Read the Before You Begin section, page 62.

2. Press and stitch a doubled 1/4" hem on the leading edge and lower edge of each panel, turning the hems toward the *right* side of the fabric.

3. Stitch a 1" double hem at the outer edge of each panel, turning to the wrong side of the fabric.

3. Piece the ruffle sections, using French seams (page 56), to the length you need.

4. Hem both edges of the ruffle. Use a narrow hemmer if you have one, or work a serger rolled hem. Or fold 1/4" to the wrong side, press, then fold the raw edge in again to the first fold line. Press, and stitch close to the inner fold.

5. Hem one end of the ruffle. It will be placed at the lower outside edge of the curtain.

6. Divide into several equal sections the edges of the curtain to which the ruffle will be attached. Divide the ruffle into an equal number of sections.

7. Gather the ruffle to fit the edges of the curtain. If you have a ruffler, you can gather the ruffle as it is sewn onto the curtain in Step 9. The gathering line will be 1" from the edge of the ruffle; the "short" ruffled edge will go toward the inner edges of the curtain. A speedy way to gather is by using a length of buttonhole gimp or crochet cotton. Hold it over the gathering line and stitch over it with a fairly long zigzag stitch. It is quicker still, and easier to guide the cord, if you adjust the needle position of your machine and use your buttonhole foot to guide the cord. In either case, be absolutely sure you don't stitch through the cord.

8. Draw up the gathers so that the marked sections of the ruffle correspond with the marked sections of the curtain edges.

9. Position the ruffle, right side up, on the right side of the curtain, the wide part of the ruffle outward and the unhemmed end at the top. The gathering line of the ruffle should be 1/4" from the edge of the curtain.

10. At the top of the curtain, release the gathers so that the ruffle is almost flat above the lower edge of the casing.

CASING ALLOWANCE

The ruffle end that extends into the casing allowance should not be gathered.

11. Stitch the ruffle just outside the cord, or gather and stitch the ruffle in place with the ruffler. Carefully remove the cord.

12. Finish the top of the curtain as in Steps 3 through 6 for the rod pocket curtain, page 62.

13. Press the stitching by holding the curtain with the stitching line just on the edge of the ironing board.

PRO tip

HAZEL WITT ▪ Interior Designer

" When selecting your window treatment, consider the view from outside the house. Hardware, lining, and style will affect the exterior appearance of your home. "

Cafe Curtains With Scalloped Tops

These little curtains are quick to make, use very little fabric, and can cheer up a room with no trouble at all. A person with even a bit of imagination can create wonderful variations with this basic style.

Cafe curtains usually consist of a single panel across the lower half of a window. They have very little fullness; width of a panel can be calculated at 1-1/3 to 1-1/2 times the window width. Allow for standard bottom and side hems. At the top, subtract 1/2" from the finished measurement, and add 5" for facing and hem.

INSTRUCTIONS BEGIN ON PAGE 73

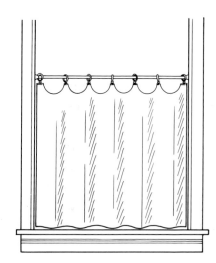

The simplicity of a cafe curtain makes it a perennial favorite for informal decorating.

Above and right: The valance, of print fabric lined in a solid color and with piping and a ruffle at one end, is simply folded over the decorative upper rod. Curtains hang from a plain rod on the window frame. Design: Ginger Kinzel

Far right: The contrasting ruffle on these curtains is sewn into the lining seam at the leading and lower edges. Placement of the tiebacks and length of the curtains give importance to the small window. Design: Kathryn Long

A curved cornice board supports the box-pleated heading of these distinctive curtains. Tiebacks are placed high to allow maximum light through the narrow windows.
Design: Donna Evans

A delicate lace sash curtain on the door between bedroom and bath complements the Victorian style of the house. The simple valance above serves to blend the colors of both rooms. Design: Kathryn Long

Top: Sheer fabric can be purchased with a patterned border, used here for a charming sash curtain and valance over French doors. Design: Kathryn Long

Center: The color of the shaped valance is repeated in the accessories in a pretty powder room. Plenty of fullness gives a rich look to both the curtain and the valance. Design: Kathryn Long

Bottom: The patterned border of the sheer fabric is used to edge a shaped two-piece valance. Valance and curtain are sewn together at the casing and used with a single rod. Design: Pat Wald

Above: Valances and stationary curtain panels unify a group of bay windows. The prominent pattern and longer valances are in just the right proportions for the size of the bay. Design: Kathryn Long

Left: Always a favorite, the cheery hourglass curtain is neatly shaped by cutting the upper and lower edges on a curve. Design: Rosaleen Feeser

Right: A curved mounting board supports these distinctive goblet-pleated curtains. Careful alignment of pattern motifs across the panels gives these elegant curtains a thoroughly professional look. Design: Ginger Kinzel

Left: A pretty alternative to sash curtains for French doors, these sheer curtains are kept in their places with decorative holdbacks so the cat can pursue his birdwatching hobby. Design: Kathryn Long

Below: The use of a single pattern creates a unified room from a variety of individual elements. Simple white half-curtains keep the room bright, while the box-pleated balloon valance continues the pattern. Design: Susan Nilsson

CONTINUED FROM PAGE 65

1. Read the Before You Begin section on page 62, then prepare and cut your fabric.

2. Work the bottom and side hems according to the detailed instructions on page 58.

3. Fold the upper edge of the curtain 1" to the wrong side; press and stitch.

4. Draw a chalk line across the fabric to represent the finished upper edge of the curtain.

5. Cut a piece of fairly stiff fusible interfacing slightly smaller all around than the upper facing.

6. Place the interfacing on the wrong side of the facing, aligning one long edge with the chalk line. Center it between the fabric edges. Fuse in place.

7. Fold the facing, on the chalk line, to the right side of the fabric, so the interfacing faces outward.

8. Figure that the scallops will be approximately 5" in diameter, and the spaces between them should be between 1/2" and 1" wide.

9. Measure the width of the curtain between the inner folds of the side hems to get the amount of space which can be used for scallops. Divide that figure by 6. Round off the result to the nearest whole number to get the number of scallops that will fit across the curtain.

10. Find a bowl or plate approximately 5" in diameter to use as a template, and a piece of kraft paper to use for patterns. Trace the outline of the bowl on the paper and cut out shapes equal in number to the scallops you need.

11. Line up the scallops along the top of the curtain, one at each side hemline, and one centered over the center point on the curtain. Fiddle with them until they fit, with equal spacing between them.

12. Trace around the circles on the interfacing with a fabric marking pen.

13. Stitch along the ink lines with a fairly short straight stitch.

14. Trim to within 1/4" of the stitching. Clip notches from the edge almost to the stitching line.

15. Turn right side out. Press. Hand-stitch the facings to the curtain at ends.

There are all sorts of ways to hang this curtain. Rings, of course, can be sewn to the tabs. Or two lengths of pretty ribbon might be sewn to each tab and tied over the rod. Or you could even use the brightly colored plastic-coated "French" clothespins to hold the curtain to the rod.

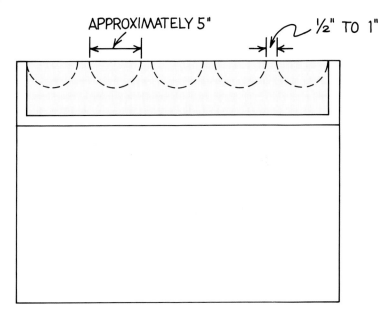

Space scallops evenly. Mark the stitching lines on the interfacing.

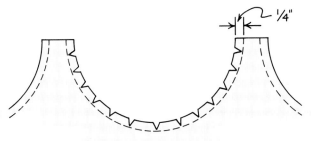

After stitching, trim and notch seam allowances.

▪ T a b   T o p   C u r t a i n   ▪

Similar to the scalloped cafe curtain in its simplicity, this curtain has tabs which are constructed separately and sewn into a facing seam at the top of the curtain. It, too, can be varied in countless ways. The tabs could be made of a contrasting fabric which could also be used to trim the lower edge of the curtain. One end of each tab might be left free and buttoned to the curtain over the rod. Or the tabs might be very long, extending up the length of the curtain from the hemline and over the rod. Tabs could be constructed of braided fabric tubes, dozens of lengths of yarn, patchwork, almost anything.

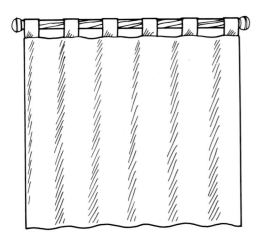

This cafe curtain variation features tabs sewn into the facing seam along the top of the curtain.

Read Before You Begin, page 62.

To measure for length of the finished curtain and the tabs, hold a tape measure over the rod and pinch it together below the rod where you want the top of the curtain to be. Allow plenty of ease for the tabs to slide along the rod. The section of the tape above that point and over the rod will be the finished length of the tabs.

This is a traditional cafe curtain in that it is meant to cover the window in a single panel. If you want a pair, simply adjust your measurements.

Allow 1-1/3 to 1-1/2 times the width for fullness. To the finished measurement, add allowances for lower and side hems, and 1/2" seam allowance at the top. Cut a piece for facing the width of the finished curtain plus 1", and 4" long.

These wider tabs look best if the space between them is slightly less than double the width of a finished tab. This tab width is proportionate to a rod about 1" in diameter. If you use a smaller rod, narrower tabs might look better.

To estimate the number of tabs you will need, divide the *cut* width of the panel by 2. Multiply the result by the number of tabs you will use, and add 1" seam allowance for each tab. Figure the total length required for tabs. Cut a strip this length and 3-1/2" wide. The strip will be seamed, then cut into tab lengths.

1. Hem the lower edge and sides of the curtain.

2. Fold the tab strip with right sides together and long raw edges aligned. Stitch 1/2" from raw edges. Turn right side out and press.

3. Cut the strip into individual tabs. Fold each tab in half.

4. Position the tabs on the right side of the curtain, ends aligned with the top of the curtain, folds extend-

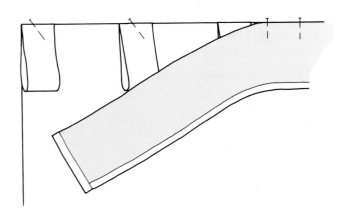

Sandwich folded tabs between the right side of the curtain and the right side of the facing.

ing toward the lower edge. Place one tab at each end, even with the hemmed edge, and space the rest evenly across the top. Stitch the tabs to the curtain, stitching 1/4" from the curtain edge.

5. Fold under 1/2" along one long edge of the facing. Press and stitch.

6. Fold under 1/2" along each end; press.

7. Position the facing at the top of the curtain, with right sides together so that the tabs are sandwiched between, raw edges aligned. Stitch across the top. Turn and press.

8. Hand-stitch the facing to the curtain at the ends.

▪ H o u r g l a s s   C u r t a i n s ▪

This shaped curtain over the glass can make a focal point of an otherwise ordinary door. Like the sash curtain, it is simply a rod pocket curtain with a casing added at the lower edge, but with the top and bottom cut on a curve. The fabric width allowed for this curtain should be 2 to 2-1/2 times the rod length.

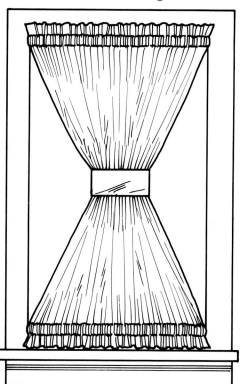

The hourglass curtain is shaped by cutting the upper and lower edges on a curve.

1. Mount the rods approximately 1" above and below the glass.

2. Determine the width of the center "waist" of the curtain, and mark each end on the window, placing the waist halfway between the upper and lower rods.

3. To determine finished length at the outer

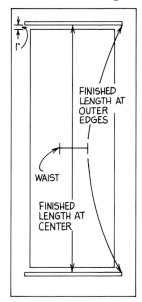

Hold the tape straight to measure the length at the center of the curtain; curve it to measure for the outer edges.

edges, hold the end of a plastic or cloth tape measure just below one end of the upper rod. Curve the tape inward to that end of the marked waist, and outward to the top of the same end of the lower rod.

4. To determine the finished length at center, measure straight from the bottom of the top rod to the top of the lower rod across the center of the marked waist.

5. Add casing allowances at the top and bottom according to the Rod Pocket Curtain instructions on page 62.

6. To cut the fabric, add the casing allowances to the outer edge length measurement. Cut the fabric to this length.

7. Stitch a doubled 1" hem on each side.

8. Fold the curtain in half lengthwise. Mark the center, top and bottom.

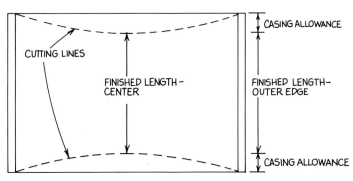

Dotted lines indicate cutting lines for the upper and lower edges.

CUTTING LINES

FINISHED LENGTH – CENTER

CASING ALLOWANCE

FINISHED LENGTH – OUTER EDGE

CASING ALLOWANCE

9. At the center marks, mark the finished center length of the curtain, centering this measurement between top and bottom of the panel. Add the casing allowance at both top and bottom; mark the panel at the centers.

10. Hold one end of a flexible metal tape at an upper corner of the panel, curve it downward to the outermost center mark, and upward again to the other corner. Draw along this line with a fabric marker. Repeat for the bottom.

11. Cut the top and bottom along the lines.

12. Sew the casings as described in the instructions for Rod Pocket Curtains, page 62.

13. Slip the rods into the casings and hang the curtain. Use a decorative cord or ribbon, or make a tieback to draw in the waist to the finished measurement.

Special Handling for Sheers

Sheer fabrics are perhaps the most popular and most adaptable choices for window coverings, and they can be made up in virtually any style window or top treatment. As curtains, they allow light to fill the room, and provide privacy at the same time. Because of their excellent draping qualities they perform well as graceful swags or scarves. They are ideal for delicate Austrian shades.

Most sheers wash beautifully—as long as the fabric is preshrunk before sewing. Sheer fabrics also have some eccentricities, and they need a little special handling during the construction process.

▪ Sheer curtains look best with plenty of fullness. Allow three times the finished width for fabric cutting width.

▪ Sheer fabrics are available in widths up to 120". It is best to use the wider fabric and avoid seams if possible.

▪ It is essential, with sheer fabrics, to pull a thread in order to cut the fabric straight across the grain. A thread should be pulled to mark the upper edge as well as the bottom of a width.

▪ Always use a perfect needle to sew sheers. A dull or damaged needle can pull threads in the fabric. Try a size 80/12 needle; some fabrics may require a smaller size.

▪ Sew with a fairly short stitch length, 10 or 12 stitches to the inch, or shorter if puckering occurs. A stitch plate with a small hole is also helpful. Hold the fabric taut while sewing.

▪ If widths of sheer fabric must be joined, use a French seam or a serger rolled hem stitch (see pages 56 and 57).

- If the selvages do not shrink or pucker when the fabric is preshrunk, they can be left intact and used in lieu of hems at the outer edges.

- The bottom hem in a sheer curtain should be wider than is customary for the style. For long curtains, a doubled 6" hem is appropriate.

- To make sure the hem is perfectly straight, pull a second thread along the fold line closest to the edge of the fabric. Hems in sheers should be stitched by hand.

- Weight the hems of sheers. Very fine weights, encased in fabric tubing, are made especially for use with sheer fabrics.

■ Sash Curtains

This tidy window treatment works especially well with sheer fabric. It is made to cover just the glass portion of a window or door, and since it is not opened or closed, only a single panel is needed. Special sash rods, encased in rod pockets at both top and bottom of the curtain, are mounted directly onto the wooden part of the door or the window sash to hold the curtain snugly against the glass.

The sash curtain is stretched between two rods or wires to hold it against the window glass.

To make a sash curtain, follow the instructions for the Rod Pocket Curtain, page 62, but add a second casing at the lower edge of the curtain. If you are using a sheer fabric, read the section above before you begin.

The rod should be installed before measuring so that the length can be calculated carefully, as this style looks best if the curtain is held taut between the rods. Mount the rods approximately 1" above and below the glass. This curtain does not need quite the fullness of sheers that hang free; figure fabric width at 2 to 2-1/2 times the finished width measurement.

■ Sheer Curtains with Shirred Heading

These sheers have deep, graceful gathers across the top and are used with traverse rods so they can be drawn open and closed with cords. Because of the heading and hem depths, they look best floor length. Mounted on the outer rod of a double, they soften the colors of the drapery behind them. Choose a lightweight, fairly soft fabric for these curtains.

To measure the window and determine yardage requirements, use the charts on page 46. Allow 14" for bottom hems. Also allow 14" for the heading. Buy 4-cord shirring tape, twice the length of the fabric width measurement plus about 8" for ease and trimming. You will also need lightweight fusible interfacing 7" wide and the length of the fabric width measurement.

Read the information about working with sheers, above.

Prepare the fabric according to the instructions on page 52. Preshrink the fabric and the heading tape if the curtains will be washed.

1. Hem the curtains and mark the upper finish line following the instructions for the pencil pleat draperies, page 93, but omit the lining steps.

2. On the wrong side of the curtain, position the interfacing on the heading allowance, aligning the lower edge of the interfacing with the finish line of

Subtle sheer curtains allow the valance the starring role in this window treatment.

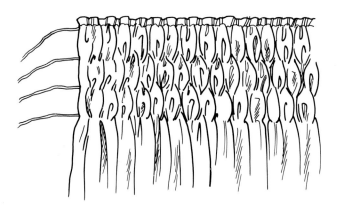

Graceful shirring on lightweight curtains can be accomplished easily with corded tape.

the curtain. Fuse the interfacing according to the manufacturer's instructions.

3. Fold the upper half of the heading allowance down to just cover the interfacing; press.

4. Fold the heading down again so that the fold line meets the finish line of the curtain top.

5. Sew on the two strips of shirring tape, gather, and finish according to the instructions for the pencil pleat draperies, page 93.

PRO tip

CHRISTINE LOFGREN ▪ Drapery Maker

" When you sew crinoline heading to sheers, the sheer tends to stretch, ending up longer at the end of a seam. To solve this problem, apply a paper-backed fusible bonding agent to the crinoline, then remove the backing and fuse it to the sheer. "

▪ Fanlight Curtain

A fitted sheer curtain accents the half-round window above a door or at the top of an arch. A choux rosette (page 140) at the center provides a nice finishing touch. The custom curved rod can be ordered through a drapery supply store. With this curtain it is especially important to install the rod before measuring.

Measure the diameter of the rod. Measure carefully from the center point to the inside edge of the rod; measure at several points and use the average

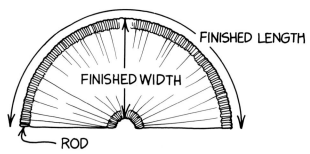

For finished length, measure from the center point to the inner edge of the rod. For width, measure the rod from end to end.

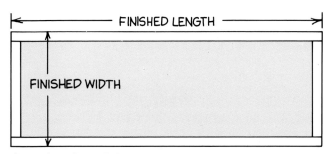

The rod is slipped through the upper curtain casing; a cord through the lower casing is used to draw up the fullness at the center of the window.

if there are differences. This will be the length of the curtain. Measure the length of the rod to determine the curtain width.

To cut fabric, allow for the rod pocket according to the instructions on page 62. At the lower edge, which will be the center point, add 1", which will be doubled for a 1/2" casing. In width, allow 2-1/2 times the circumference measurement for fullness, and add 4" for side hems.

1. Stitch the side hems; the finished width is 1".

2. Make the rod casing, following the directions on page 62.

3. To make the lower casing, fold the raw edge 1" to the wrong side; press. Fold the raw edge in by 1/2"; press and stitch.

4. Attach a small safety pin to a length of cord several inches longer than the curtain width; thread it through the lower casing.

5. Slip the curtain onto the rod and adjust fullness. Draw up the cord at the center, as tightly as possible. Tie the cord and tuck the ends away. Add the choux rosette if you wish.

DRAPERIES

Long draperies are an elegant and practical window treatment which will serve for many years. They open and close easily to provide excellent light control and privacy, and their ample fabric softens a room's lines while insulating against both heat and cold.

Planning and Preparing

Before you measure for your draperies, decide upon the rod style you will use and the rod length you need. Correct rod length is determined by the finished width of the panels, and by the amount of space the drapery panels occupy when they are drawn open, or the *stackback*. Allowing for stackback when figuring rod length means that the glass of the window will be fully exposed when the curtains are open.

Determining Rod Length

For lined draperies of medium-weight fabric, with standard pleating, total stackback can be estimated at one third the width of the window glass. Allow half this amount at each side of the window for two-way draw draperies. For draperies with one-way draw, subtract approximately 6". If your fabric is quite heavy, add 1" per width of fabric used. Add the total stackback to the width of the window opening to determine the length your rod should be. With traverse rods, be sure that this rod length will allow the master slides to clear the window glass area when drawn open.

Figuring Finished Length

The rod should, if at all possible, be installed before you measure; your measurement is more likely to be accurate. If you cannot install the rod first, mark its position very carefully before you measure.

First decide where the bottom of the drapery will be. For floor-length draperies, 1/2" above the floor or carpet is standard. If the room has thick or shaggy carpet, place a piece of thin, stiff cardboard on the floor for more accurate measuring. Draperies can also be apron length, ending just below the window frame. If you have a radiator or furniture beneath the window, you might prefer that the draperies end just above that object. Experiment with a sheet to find the best length.

With a conventional traverse rod, measure from 1/2" above the top of the rod. If you are using a decorator traverse rod, measure from the pinholes in the slides. Measure from the screw eye at the bottom

RETURN

3¾"

4"

STACKBACK

LEADING EDGE

OUTER EDGE

Allow for stackback when determining rod length so draperies will clear the glass area when opened.

of a ring for a rod with rings. In the case of the latter two, you may be able to measure more accurately if you thread a weighted string through the pinhole, let it drop to the chosen length, then measure the string.

For a ceiling-mounted rod, measure from 1/4" below the top of the rod.

▪ Choosing a Heading Style

The method used to gather in fullness at the top of the draperies affects the cut length of the panels. With pleated headings you also need to decide the depth of the heading. With floor-length draperies, a 4" heading is standard; a 3" heading would look good with shorter styles. With a heavy, rich fabric such as brocade or velvet, or with extra-long draperies, you might want a heading 5 or 6" deep. The deeper heading is not strictly decorative; a wider interfacing also helps support the weight of long or heavy draperies. Look through the photographs, and look at the descriptions of the different heading styles in this section to help you decide what you would like to do. The chart shows the heading allowance to use in calculating your fabric yardage.

Heading Allowance

Heading style	Heading material	Heading allowance
Pinch pleats or Goblet pleats	4" crinoline	
	4" or buckram	8"
	3" crinoline	
	4" or buckram	6"
	4" pleater tape	4-1/2"
	3" pleater tape	3-1/2"
Pencil pleats	3-1/4" tape	4"
Box pleats	4" crinoline	
	4" or buckram	8"

▪ Hem Allowances

Generally speaking, the finished bottom hem of a drapery should be the same depth as the heading, and it should always be doubled. So if you are using 4" crinoline for the heading, add 8" for a hem allowance at the lower edge.

Side hems also should be doubled. A finished hem of 1-1/2" is a good size, which means adding 3" to each side of the panel as the hem allowance. If the fabric is very heavy, add an additional 1/2" to each hem allowance.

▪ Fabric Yardage Requirements

Read through the specific instructions for the heading you are using; there may be other considerations that will affect yardage. You should now have the facts you need to figure the amount of face fabric for your draperies. Use the figures from this section with the charts on page 46 to calculate your yardage.

▪ How Much Lining?

Use the finished length measurement to determine the length of lining fabric you will need. Add 3" for hem allowance at the lower edge and 1" ease allowance at the top.

If your drapery panels will contain more than one width of fabric, it will be easier to figure lining width requirements if you sew the vertical seams in the outer fabric first. Then decide which method you will use to attach the lining to the face fabric.

If you use the Pro Method (page 89), the lining should be cut 1" wider on each side than the finished measurement of the panel. Add to this 1" for each seam if you are using more than one fabric width per panel.

If you use a Sack Lining (page 89), cut the lining 2" narrower on each side than the finished width measurement, again making sure that any vertical seams in the lining correspond with those in the face

Right and far right: A window design challenge is deftly handled with the use of plantation shutters above rich linen draperies and sheer curtains. The fringed, box-pleated valance hangs from a mounting board and is topped with the linen to present a neat appearance from above. Design: Drew Atkinson

Below: In a distinctive cornice and valance combination, the shirred cornice cover sports thick corded piping along the top and at the valance seamline. Placement of the pattern motifs was planned with care. Design: Drew Atkinson

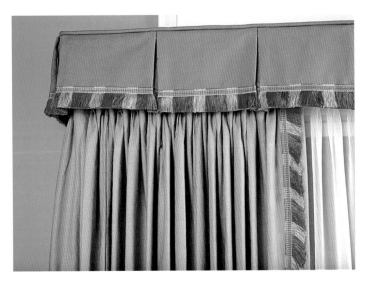

Left: A bold wooden rod and extra fabric length perfectly suit the bright, splashy pattern of these draperies. The designer painted the grooves in the rod lavender, for a simple decorative touch. Design: Kathryn Long

Top: A nicely proportioned shirred swag with jabots tops the sheer curtains and draperies. Design: Drew Atkinson

Above: The rippled lower edge of the valance adds linear interest with draperies that cover a wide expanse of window. Design: Rosaleen Feeser

In an unexpected variation of a traditional treatment, outer draperies here are made of double width sheer fabric with a patterned border. Behind are plain white draperies which can be drawn for nighttime privacy. Design: Ruby Haynes

fabric. If you figure width based on a 3" hem allowance for the outer fabric, using the sack lining will add a total of 3" to the width of the panel.

Whenever possible, buy lining fabric the same width as your outer fabric. Seams in the lining should correspond with seams in the face fabric if it is necessary to piece the panels, otherwise a lining seamline can show through to the right side of the drapery, and with pressing and wear can mark the face fabric.

▪ Should You Interline?

An interlining serves two functions: It can enhance the face fabric, adding body, opacity, and a luxurious quality to the finished drapery; and it can provide additional insulation. For added body, a stable, lightweight fabric such as a cotton/polyester or all cotton batiste is a good choice. It is important that the interlining fabric be compatible with the outer fabric because the two will serve as a single unit once the drapery is constructed. The interlining should be lighter in weight than the face fabric; it should be less stiff and just as stable.

If an interlining will be used for its thermal properties, there are good fabrics available for the purpose from manufacturers of lining fabrics. Keep in mind that a thermal lining will add considerably to the "heaviness" of the outer fabric, resulting in a somewhat thicker appearance of the finished draperies.

To determine the amount of interlining to buy, add 1" all around to the finished measurements of the drapery panel. If it will be necessary to use more than one width of fabric in a panel, seams in the interlining must correspond to those in the face fabric, as with lining.

▪ Heading Materials

Use the width of the panels to determine the amount of heading tape or stiffener to buy. With buckram or crinoline, allow about 2" extra, per panel, for trimming and turning under at the ends. If you use self-pleating tape, buy an extra 10" per panel.

Standard buckram and crinoline made for drapery headings are not washable. If you intend to wash your draperies, consult with store personnel to find a washable heading interfacing that's compatible with your fabric. Then preshrink the heading material with your fabric.

▪ Preparing and Cutting Your Fabric

Take the time to properly prepare your fabrics before you cut. It takes a little work to straighten and square your fabric before you begin, but by doing it now you will prevent problems later. If you plan to wash your draperies, be sure to preshrink all your materials—headings included—before you cut (see page 52).

Cut your materials according to the instructions on page 53. A rotary cutter, used with its companion cutting mat and a long, sturdy plastic ruler, can save considerable time and produce perfectly straight edges. If you haven't investigated these tools, a drapery-making project is the perfect opportunity to try them.

▪ Making the Draperies ▪

Read about seams and seam finishing options in the Basic Techniques section (page 54) before you begin. After each seam is sewn, press the stitching line to work the stitches into the fabric, then press the seam allowances according to the seam finish you are using.

Many professionals make a lined drapery following this sequence. Specific instructions for your drapery style may call for a slightly different order of work.

1. Stitch together vertical sections of panel if necessary.

2. Apply the interlining, if desired.

3. Stitch bottom and side hems in the face fabric, and the bottom hem in the lining.

4. Apply lining to face fabric.

5. Interlock the lining to the face fabric.

6. Stitch the heading and make pleats.

7. Hang the draperies and tend to finishing details.

■ Joining the Widths

If your panels are made up of more than one width of fabric, stitch the vertical seams first. If a panel contains a half width of fabric, place the half width at the outer edge of the panel, and, for two-way draw draperies, be sure you make a left and a right panel. For the specifics on matching patterns, see page 58.

■ Interlining

If you are using an interlining, attach it to the face fabric at this point. Place the face fabric wrong side up on the table and place the interlining on top. The face fabric should extend beyond the interlining by 2" at each side, and by 7" at the lower edge. Allow 1" for each vertical seam required to piece the widths.

Seams in the interlining should correspond to seams in the outer fabric. In interlining, seam the widths by overlapping the seam allowances and stitching up the center of the overlap with a multiple step zigzag stitch, if your machine has one, set with a fairly long stitch length and at maximum possible width. If you use a regular zigzag stitch, use the longest stitch you can use without the fabric puckering, and the maximum width setting. Press the stitching line well.

If the interlining fabric does not want to cling to the outer fabric you may want to secure the two layers by lockstitching them together. Follow the instructions on page 90. Place the first vertical row of lockstitching about 12" from one side and space the rows about 18" apart across the panel.

Start the rows of stitching approximately 6" below the top of the interfacing, working to within 2" of the lower edge.

Fold back 1" along the lower edge, so that the fold is just at the hemline and the seam allowance uppermost. Press. Stitch to the face fabric at the hemline with long catchstitches, beginning and ending an inch from each edge.

Fold back 1" along a side in the same way. Press, and catchstitch, stitching to within 1" of the top and lower edge. Repeat for the other side. Clip the ends of the seam allowance at the lower corners at a diagonal toward the corner, so that they will lie flat without overlapping.

■ Bottom Hems

Detailed instructions for hemming are on page 58. Bottom hems are usually stitched first, but if you are unsure of your measurements, your skills, or your fabric, you may wish to baste the lower hems until you have hung the draperies. If this is the way you go, also baste the lower part of the side hems in both the face fabric and lining, then stitch them permanently after you have permanently stitched the bottom hems.

■ Lining

The method you choose for lining depends on your fabrics and the amount of time you are willing to devote to these draperies. As with most projects, the more time-consuming method will produce the most attractive finished product.

With the Pro Method, the lining is sewn to the side seams of the drapery panel by hand. The advantage to this is that whenever two different fabrics are joined, each will change slightly with age and because of hanging, and sooner or later there will be stretching or puckering along a machine-sewn seam. Stitching by hand allows slight ease along the seamline, and the fabrics can adjust themselves without affecting the look of the drapery.

With the Sack Method, the lining is machine-sewn to the face fabric at both edges. This method can work well if the lining and face fabrics are similar in weight and stability, as firmly woven cotton is used for both face and lining. It will not work well with two very different fabrics; cotton lining used with a rayon and cotton damask, for example. This method cannot be used if you plan to interlock the drapery to an interlining all across the width of the panel.

Whichever lining method you use, handle the pieces carefully after you have aligned the two layers of fabric for stitching.

Professional Lining Method

Read the section on hems, page 58, before you begin.

- Finish bottom hems of the fabric and the lining.
- Finish both side hems in the outer fabric by hand or with a machine blind stitch.
- Fold, press and pin side hems in the lining.
- Place the lining on the finished panel with wrong sides together. Carefully align the pieces so that the edges of the lining are 1" inside the edges of the outer panel, and the lower edge of the lining is 1" above the lower edge of the drapery panel.

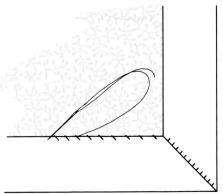

After stitching lining to the outer drapery fabric at the sides, hand-stitch the lining hem to the drapery hem for a distance of about 6" in from each edge.

- Pin the two layers together along the top and bottom and along the outer edge. Then work the interlocking as described on page 90.
- Along the sides, hand-stitch the lining to the drapery panel side hem allowance, catching the folded

edge of the lining and just the one thickness of the drapery fabric.

- Loosely stitch the lining hemline to the drapery hem for a distance of about 6" in from each side.
- Now proceed with the heading.

Sack Lining

Read the section on hems, page 58, before you begin.

- Finish bottom hems of the fabric and of the lining.
- With right sides together, align the lining with the drapery panel so that the leading edges are even and the lower hem of the drapery extends 1" below the lower hem of the lining.

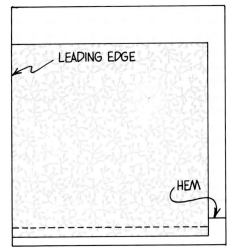

Align the leading edges of the drapery and lining to stitch them together.

- Pin the pieces together along the leading edge. Stitch the seam, using 1/2" seam allowance. Finish the seam, if desired, and press seam allowances toward the lining.
- Turn the panel right side out. Place on the table and align the layers so that the raw edge of the drapery extends 1" beyond the raw edge of the lining at the outer edge, and the seam is 1" inside the

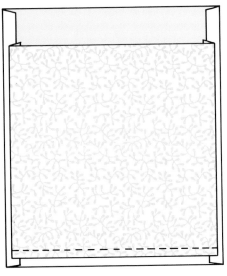

After stitching the inner edges, turn the panel right side out and position so that the side extensions of the face fabric are equal on both sides.

fold line of the drapery panel at the leading edge. Pin the lining to the drapery from top finish line to hemline about 12" from the seam.

•Carefully fold back the lining raw edge to the pins and work the line of interlocking stitch as explained in Step 5 of the general instructions.

•Carefully turn the panel wrong side out again, and align the outer raw edges of the drapery and lining, with the lower hems positioned as in Step 2 above.

•Pin, stitch, and finish as for the leading edge seam described above. Turn the panel right side out.

▪ I n t e r l o c k i n g   t h e   L i n i n g   t o   t h e   F a c e   F a b r i c

A single vertical row of interlocking stitch about 12" in from the leading edge of the panel will keep the lining from showing itself around the leading edge of the drapery.

With the panel face down on the table, fold back the lining to a point about 12" from the leading edge. The direction you fold the lining depends upon which lining method you are using. It is helpful to fold the lining fabric over a yardstick to keep the fold straight.

Thread a needle with thread to match the outer fabric. About 8" below the point where the top of the finished panel will be, take a stitch through the

lining and one thread of the face fabric. Take a second stitch 4 to 5" away from the first, leaving quite a bit of slack in the first stitch. Then pass the needle around the thread at this end of the first stitch and back up under the new, short stitch to make a kind of knot, as shown in the illustration. Continue, making sure the long stitches are very loose, to within about 8" of the hemline.

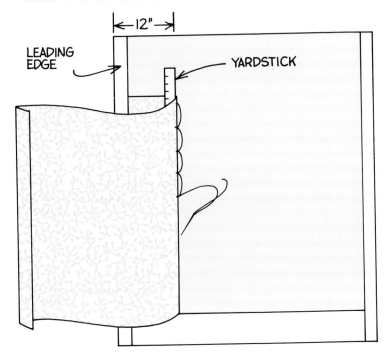

Fold back the lining to interlock the lining to the face fabric, spacing stitches 4" or 5" apart.

Detail of interlocking stitch. Leave the thread slack between stitches.

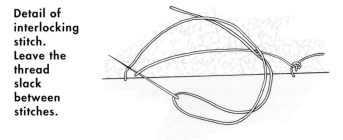

▪ T h e   H e a d i n g

To prepare the panel for the heading, place it right side down on the table, smooth it well, measure carefully from the hem to the finish point, and mark the lining at that point. If the entire panel will not fit your table, work from one side of the panel to the other, keeping the excess folded neatly and evenly. When you have marked all the way across, turn the fabric so all, or most, of the panel top is on the table. Join the marks, and carefully cut the lining (and interlining) along this line. Instructions for the specific heading styles follow.

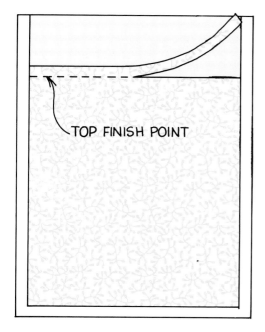

TOP FINISH POINT

Trim the lining fabric neatly along the finished top line of the drapery.

Pinch Pleated Heading

Pinch pleats are a beautiful, traditional heading for the top of a drapery. The best results are obtained by using crinoline or buckram to stiffen the heading, the chosen method of professional drapery-makers. While self-pleating tape eliminates most of the pleat arithmetic, the pleats are not as crisp, and the tape does not offer as much support for the weight of very heavy draperies as does the standard heading. With pleater tape, the hooks cannot be adjusted upward or downward on the heading to allow minor adjustments to the drapery length, so it may be a good idea to baste the lower hems until the draperies have been hung. Instructions for finishing the heading with pleater tape are on page 93.

Finishing the Upper Edge

- Fold under each end of the strip of heading stiffener

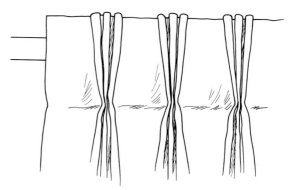

Pinch pleat heading

so that the folds are about 1/8" from the edges of the panel. Trim the ends to within about 1" of the folds.

- Place it above the lining edge on the wrong side of the drapery panel, aligning the lower edge of the stiffener with the edge of the lining, the finish point of the panel. The folded edges of the crinoline should come within 1/8" of the edges of the panel. Pin in place near the lower edge.

- Fold the upper hem allowance of the drapery fabric down over the stiffener. Press to crease the fold.

- Remove pins. Fold over once again. The new fold should be just at the upper edge of the lining.

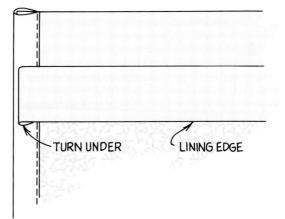

TURN UNDER **LINING EDGE**

Position the lower edge of the stiffener along the upper edge of the lining. Fold the upper edge of the face fabric over the stiffener, then fold both layers down toward the lining.

Press. Pin, placing the pins perpendicular to the lower folded edge of the heading.

- Stitch the ends across the width of the heading, positioning the stitching lines to line up with the hemlines. Backstitch securely at the ends of the seams. Stitch again very close to the edge.

91

Measuring for the Pleats

Drapery pleat arithmetic has reduced more than one intelligent person with several college degrees to a whining, pitiful wreck. It does not have to be that way. It is not difficult. Get a pencil and paper, a small calculator, perhaps a glass of very dry sherry, and you can conquer this in about ten minutes.

Generally, a pinch pleat should incorporate 4 to 6" of fabric. And *generally*, the space between pleats should approximately equal the amount of overlap at center front. Many decorators suggest an uneven number of pleats per panel.

If the steps below don't give you exactly these numbers, do not worry.

- Determine the number of pleats. If your fabric width is 45 to 54", allow 5 pleats per fabric width in the panel. Add 2 to 3 pleats for a half width.
- Figure the number of spaces at one less than the number of pleats.
- If your treatment consists of two panels for the window, subtract half your total finished width (rod length plus returns plus overlap) from the width of the flat panel. If you have one panel, subtract the full finished width from the width of the panel.
- Divide the result of Step 3 by the number of pleats. This is the amount of fabric allowed for each pleat. Round off to the nearest 1/2".
- With a two-panel drapery: For each panel, add 4" to the rod return length. Subtract this total from half the finished width. With a single panel, subtract twice the rod return length from the finished width.
- Divide this total by the number of spaces between pleats. This is the amount of space between pleats. Round off to the nearest 1/4". If you rounded down in calculating pleat size, you may need to round up in this step.
- Check your arithmetic:
    Multiply your pleat size by the number of pleats.
    Multiply the number of spaces between pleats by the size of each space.

Add these two figures.
Add to this the rod return length and the overlap.

If this total will give you panels a few inches wider than your calculated finished width, that's fine. If this total indicates that your panels will be narrower than your finished width, it would be a good idea to re-calculate.

Marking the Pleats on the Heading

If you feel your eye is more trustworthy than your math, cut paper templates equal in number and width to your calculated pleats, and lay them out across the heading before you mark the fabric. If you have vertical seams,

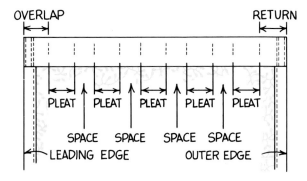

adjust the pleats, if you can, so each seam will be inside a pleat.

Keep left and right panels straight in your mind if they are different. Place one of them face down on the table. Measuring from the outside edge of one panel, place a mark the distance of the return length. From the leading edge, mark the distance which represents the overlap length. These marks are the outer edges of two pleats. Now mark pleats and spaces across the fabric, or position your paper templates, then mark the fabric if the spacing works out correctly. Readjust if necessary. Make a good, straight line at each mark, exactly perpendicular to the top of the panel and extending the width of the heading. Place an X between each pair of lines that represent spaces so you can keep them straight.

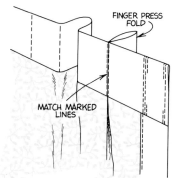

Bring the pleat lines together on the inside and stitch on the outside from top to bottom of heading.

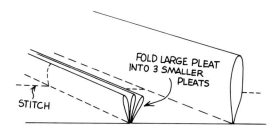

Crease the pleat on the outside. Hold the crease and press down to the stitching line to create another pleat on each side of the first pleat.

Stitching the Pleats

▪Bring two pleat marks together on the wrong side of the heading to form a pleat on the right side. Crease the fold lightly with your fingers.

▪Chalk-mark the stitching line on the right side by measuring in from the fold by half the pleat allowance measurement. Stitch the pleat from the right side, the width of the heading, backstitching securely at the ends. Repeat for the remaining pleats.

▪With the heading face up on the table, pinch the center crease of a pleat with your fingers and thumb and press down to the pleat seam so that another pleat is formed on each side of the original. Crease the two new pleats so that all three are even.

▪Stitch through the base of the pleat, just below the lower edge of the heading, from the pleat stitching line toward the folds of the pleat, stopping about 1/4" short of the outer edge of the pleat. You will need a size 14 or 16 needle in your machine for this step, and unless your machine is quite powerful you may need to stitch the pleats by hand.

Pinch Pleats With Pleater Tape

▪Make the draperies through the lining step, pages 87-90.

▪Position the panel right side up on the table. Place the tape face down on the panel (the pleat pocket openings are visible on the right side of the tape). Align the top of the tape with the top of the fabric, making sure

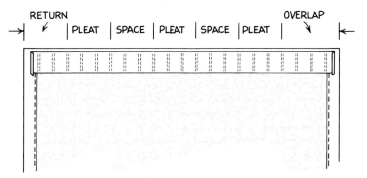

Follow the woven stitching guide to sew the tape to the panel.

that the pocket openings are at the bottom of the tape.

▪Arrange the tape so that a pleat pocket is positioned the same distance from outer edge as the return length, and one is the same distance from the leading edge as the overlap length. Count the pockets for pleats, and the spaces between, and shift the tape as necessary.

▪Cut away the ends, leaving 1/2" of tape extending beyond each edge of the panel. Fold the ends to the wrong side; press.

▪Stitch the tape to the panel along the top, following the seamline indicated on the tape. Turn, and press the seam slightly toward the wrong side.

▪Stitch the tape to the panel along the lower edge of the tape. Stitch the ends.

▪With the hook lock down, insert the hooks into the pockets. Then press the hook locks up to secure the hooks. Use a standard pin at each end of the panel.

Pencil Pleat Heading

Pencil pleats make an attractive heading and require no pleat arithmetic. As tape is used instead of a stiffening, this heading should not be used for very heavy panels.

- Make the drapery panels through the lining step, pages 87-90.
- Fold the upper hem allowance to the wrong side; press the fold. Trim to 2-3/4".

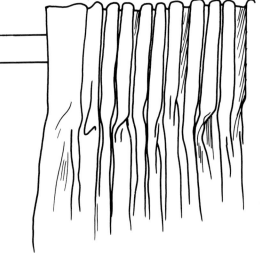

Attractive pencil pleats are easily made using a corded heading tape.

- Position the tape over the folded hem with the upper edge of the tape approximately 1/8" below the folded edge of the panel.
- At the leading edge of the panel, free the cords from the end of the tape to just inside the edge of the panel. Trim the excess tape at the end to 1/2". Fold under the end and press.
- Stitch the upper edge of the tape to the panel, following the stitching line on the tape. When you are within about 8" of the other edge, free the cords, trim, and fold under as at the beginning. Finish the stitching.
- Stitch the lower edge of the tape to the panel.
- Stitch across the ends, keeping the cords free.
- Clamp one edge of the panel securely to the table and pull the cords—all at the same time—to gather the fullness until the panel is the correct width.
- Knot the cords *tightly* together at the leading edge, and tie them loosely at the outside edge so the pleats can be adjusted later if necessary.

Heading With Goblet Pleats

This is an unusual variation of pinch pleats, no more difficult to do, and very elegant.

- Make the drapery panels through the lining step, pages 87-90. Finish the upper edge as for the pinch pleated heading, page 91.

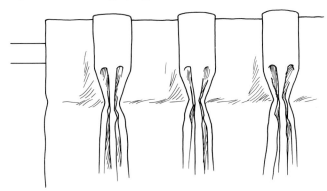

Goblet pleats are made like pinch pleats, but are not creased.

- Calculate the number of pleats and spaces between them, following the instructions on page 92. Goblet pleats look best when the pleat allowance is between 4-1/2" and 5", and when they are fairly close together. Adjust the pleat calculations accordingly.
- Mark the pleats as described on page 92.
- Bring two pleat marks together on the wrong side of the heading to form a pleat on the right side. Take care not to crease the fold.

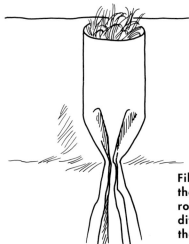

Fiberfill stuffing gives the goblet pleat a neatly rounded shape. For a different look, flatten the pleats on the front.

- To mark the stitching line on the right side, stick a pin through the top of the heading at the point where the pleat marks meet. Put another pin through at this point on the bottom of the heading. Draw a chalk line between the pins.

▪ Stitch the pleat from the right side, the width of the heading, backstitching securely at the ends. Repeat for the remaining pleats.

▪ With the heading face up on the table, pinch the center crease *just at the base of the heading* so that another pleat is formed on each side of the original. Take care not to crease the upper part of the pleat.

▪ Stitch through the base of the pleat, just below the lower edge of the heading, from the pleat stitching line toward the folds of the pleat, stopping about 1/4" short of the outer edge of the pleat. You will need a size 14 or 16 needle in your machine for this step, and unless your machine is quite powerful you may need to stitch the pleats by hand.

▪ Form the pleats. Round them, or flatten the fronts if you prefer.

▪ Stuff the pleats firmly with fiberfill to keep them in shape.

Heading With Box Pleats

The long vertical lines of box-pleated draperies can give the room an illusion of height. The tailored look of the heading can be softened by draping a decorative cord across the width at the base of the pleats, or could be enhanced with the addition of a tab at the meeting point of the pleat edges.

The width measurement calculation is slightly different for a box-pleated heading. To figure finished width, multiply the rod length by three, then add for

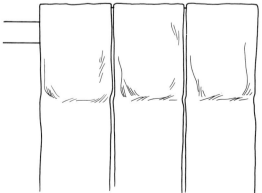

Box pleats give draperies a smoother, more tailored look.

returns and overlap. Add allowances for seams and hems to this figure to determine the number of widths needed in each panel.

▪ Make the drapery panels according to the instructions on pages 87 through 90.

▪ Finish the upper edge as for the pinch pleated heading, page 91.

▪ Calculate the pleats. The pleats are 4" wide and the spaces between are 2". There are an equal number of pleats and spaces. To figure the number of pleats and spaces for each panel of a two-panel

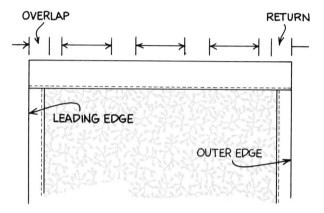

To make box pleats, crease on the outside at each marked line and bring crease to center of each pleat.

treatment, divide the straight part of the rod, excluding the overlap, by 4. Round off to the next lower whole number.

▪ Mark the pleats. Start at the leading edge. Measure in the distance of the overlap plus 2". This point is the outer edge of the first pleat.

▪ From the outside edge of the panel, measure in the distance of the return plus 2". This is the outer edge of a pleat.

▪ The remaining space should divide into 6" increments; one pleat and one space each.

▪ If you would like to verify the measurements before marking the fabric, use paper templates as described on page 92. If there is a seam in the panel, try to space the pleats so it will be inside one of them.

▪ Mark and stitch the pleats as described on pages 92-93.

- Flatten the pleats and center each one over its seamline.

- Stitch the edges of the pleats to the heading near the top and at the base. You will need a size 14 or 16 needle in your machine for this step, and unless your machine is quite powerful you may need to tack the pleats by hand.

▪ Hanging & Finishing ▪

When the calculating and sewing are finished, and your beautiful new draperies are ready to go on the window, call in another pair of hands—and another pair of admiring eyes.

For headings made with interior stiffening, the placement of hooks in the heading depends upon the rod you are using. With conventional traverse rods, the top of the hook loop should be approximately 1-3/4" inches from the top of the panel. For a decorator traverse rod the loop should be 3/4" to 1" from the top, and for a decorator rod with rings, about 1" from the top.

Test the hook placement before you insert—then have to relocate—all of them. Starting at the leading edge of the drapery, position several hooks and try it on the rod, having your assistant hold the other end of the drapery to support the weight. When you are pleased with the height of the drapery top, insert a hook securely behind each pleat and about 1/2" from each end, making sure the point doesn't protrude to the front.

If you basted the lower hem in place, wait a week before adjusting it. Take down the draperies and stitch the permanent hem. Then loosely stitch the lining to the outer drapery at the hemline for a distance of about 6" in from each edge.

The draperies need to be trained to hang neatly. Open the panels as far as they will go. Arrange the pleats so they fall perfectly straight and in even folds from the heading. Tie a strip of cloth around the panel about a third of the way down from the heading, just tight enough to keep it in place, but not so tight that the

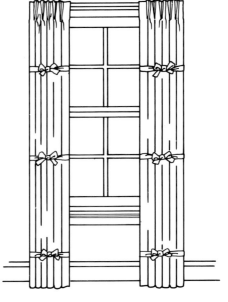

Tie the new drapery panels with strips of cloth (thin cord or string might mark the fabric) to train the pleats.

panel is drawn in. Tie a second strip around the panel a third of the way up from the bottom, and another in between. Leave them for several days, if you can.

▪ Detachable Lining

A separate lining can provide additional insulation in winter, then be removed for the summer months. There are several different thermal fabrics available which would work well.

For the heading, use a special double-faced tape made for the purpose if you can locate it. Otherwise, use a double-cord shirring tape.

Base the width of the lining on the width of the drapery heading. Add hem allowances, and add 1/2" ease for each drapery pleat. In length this lining should be 2" shorter than the drapery.

Hem the lower edge and sides of the drapery lining according to one of the methods on page 58. Attach the heading. Draw up the heading cords so that the top of the lining is shorter by 1" than the top of the drapery. With standard hooks, attach the lining to the lower edge of the drapery heading between the pleats and at the ends. To keep the lining and drapery together at the edges, stitch the lining to the drapery down the sides with fairly loose stitches.

At the hemline, loosely stitch the lining to the face fabric for about 6" in from each edge.

TOP TREATMENTS

The element of a window treatment above the draperies or curtains provides the crowning touch; it completes the design begun by the more functional elements of the treatment below.

A double-layer valance, shaped and piped along the outer edges, provides contrast to the wooden blind while maintaining the simplicity of line. Design: Pam Long

Above: An elongated cornice, covered with fabric and trimmed with contrasting piping, frames a garden view. Design: Donna Evans

Left: Two valance styles alternate to dress a long expanse of window without detracting from the spectacular scenery beyond. At the left and right, a simple lined valance is stuffed with tissue to give it dimension. The center valance, in the print used to trim its companions, is shirred onto two rods which are spaced to allow a little fullness to the fabric. Design: Donna Williams

This simple valance on a wide cornice rod makes good use of the fabric design. The separate casing is cut along the lengthwise grain, while the heading and lower section are cut crosswise. Design: Donna Evans

In a print that emphasizes the wallpaper design, this valance features box pleats planned around the pattern motifs. Design: Donna Evans

Above left: Ample fabric width and lining give this shaped valance its luxuriant look. Design: Kathryn Long

Left: In this charming design, valance and jabots are cut as a single piece. Solid green is used for lining and as trim along the lower edge. Design: Drew Atkinson

Right: Separate fabric shapes, each lined and folded, are sewn to a heading to create this imaginative valance. Design: Donna Evans

Top left: A stained glass picture flanked by plants and topped by a simple length of lace creates a personalized window treatment. Design: Donna Williams

Top right: Careful pattern placement on a padded cornice balances the graceful bias-cut edges of the jabots below. Design: Dianne Ingle

Above: The balloon shade provides a pleasant contrast to the accordion blind underneath. Design: Ruby Haynes

Right: A balloon valance, ruffled at the lower edge, combines with a fabric screen for a most imaginative window covering. Design: Kathryn Long

An effective top treatment can result from the simplest design and a very special fabric. Here, a rectangle of tapestry print, shaped at the ends, is lined with a solid color and trimmed with fringe. The finished piece is simply folded over a spring tension rod set into the window frame. Design: Donna Evans

Above: Linen scarves, edged with delicate cutwork embroidery, are just the right accent for these dining room windows. Design: Debbie Denton

Left: In a creative combination of fabrics, this lace valance is lined with polished cotton for a pleasant contrast with the mini blinds below. Design: Kathryn Long

Right: A simple curtain, artfully arranged, adds an interesting shape above a kitchen window. Design: Donna Evans

The formal design of this window treatment complements the sophisticated patterns and colors of the fabric. Crowning the double swag is a fabric rose which repeats the pattern motif to complete the design. Design: Pam Long

Left: An elegant frame for a pretty view, long jabots are lined in a coordinating solid color to offset the carefully draped swag. Design: Gail Britt

Top: Simple fabric scarves provide a creative dressing for fan lights and serve to unify the dissimilar windows in this comfortable room. Design: Kathryn Long

Above: A shaped valance, in fabric printed to match the wallpaper, softens the look of the purchased shutters below. Design: Kathryn Long

Right: A delicate pouf valance, its lower edge supported by a rod hidden underneath, dresses up a plain roller shade, which offers privacy. Design: Donna Williams

Above: Crisp polished cotton gives this Austrian valance its fullness. It is made with a casing and heading, and with a double ruffle at the lower and outer edges. Design: Donna Williams

Left: Graceful lines and beautiful proportions make this window treatment a success. The thick rod has a shirred fabric cover, with the swag draped and knotted above. Design: Dianne Ingle

A top treatment may be either decorative or functional, covering unattractive rods and hardware or camouflaging frames and trim that are not quite level. It can serve as a repeat of what goes below, like a valance which duplicates the style and shape of the curtains beneath it, or it can provide a contrast, such as a gracefully draped swag above a tailored Roman shade. The top treatment is effective in giving the room a sense of proportion and balance by drawing the eye to a higher or lower point. It can add height to the window, or widen it. It may soften lines in the room, or add a missing color or shape to the decor. And sometimes a top treatment is the only thing a window needs.

The wonderfully practical purchased window treatments—mini blinds, cellular blinds, vertical blinds, and louvered shutters—sometimes are difficult to blend into a traditional or casual decorating scheme. A carefully planned top treatment can help them make the transition, and can add your own personal style note at the same time. Since the lines of shutters and blinds are either horizontal or vertical, a top treatment with the opposite linear orientation can lessen the effect of the blinds. A simple valance with mini blinds will give height to the window. A draped swag with vertical blinds will counter the vertical lines. With either, a fabric-covered cornice can maintain the simplicity of the shade yet soften the overall effect.

A top treatment should be planned as a part of the overall window treatment, not added as an afterthought. The considerations of design and function affect what goes above the rod as much as the lower part of the treatment. However, if you don't have much experience with window treatment design and construction, it may be best to leave the final design details and construction of the top treatment until the draperies or shades are in place.

Top treatments come in three basic styles: a structured cornice, the softer valance, or draped swags and scarves. There are unlimited variations and combinations of these, and of the ways they can be used.

Cornices

A cornice is a constructed top treatment, a rigid structure most often made of plywood, sometimes with shaping on the face, and usually mounted above the window frame. It can be painted, or padded and covered with fabric. It can serve as a support for an elaborate top treatment such as swags or stationary panels, or it may simply serve as a covering for drapery rigging.

A cornice should be planned as part of the overall window treatment. But it is much easier to figure the size if the final measurements are made after the main part of the window treatment is in place. Then make a cardboard or paper mock-up and tape it in place to be sure the proportions are right, and the height correct.

A solid cornice may be painted, or covered with fabric.

Simple Cornice

To make a simple cornice, you need 1" pine for the top and legs, according to measurements; 1/4" interior grade plywood for the face; finishing nails; white glue; a saw; and a hammer. For mounting: small angle irons; screws; anchors, depending upon your wall construction; a screwdriver.

Measure for the top first. In width, it should measure the width of the curtain or drapery rod, or of the window frame if it will top a shade, plus 3 to 4" at each side to allow for the fabric of the draperies. The depth, or projection, depends on the rod too. Over a standard rod, 6" is an average; a projection of about 3" beyond the rod. Used with a double rod, projection might be 8 to 10". Again, be sure that it will allow free movement of the fabric below it. With a plain shade, a 4" projection should be enough; a full Austrian shade might require slightly more space.

The ends, or legs, will measure in width the same as the projection of the top. The length depends on

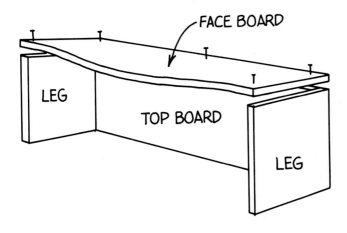

The legs are first attached to the top, then the face board is put in place.

the proportion of the cornice to the curtains or draperies, but will generally be from 4 to 8". This is where the mock-up is helpful; the cornice shouldn't overpower the lower treatment, nor should it be dwarfed by it.

The face board—the front of the cornice—will not support weight, so it can be made of the lighter plywood, or even of particle board or foam core if it is to be shaped. Cut it the width of the top board. In height, it measures the height of the legs plus the thickness of the top.

Attach the top to the legs first. Glue it in place, then nail. Then glue and nail the face.

If the cornice will be covered with fabric, it is a good idea to paint the inside to match the window trim. It will look better, and paint will protect the wood.

■ Covered Cornice

A fabric-covered cornice looks better with a little padding under the cloth. Use 1" fiberfill batting for this. Cut the batting about 1-1/2" wider all around than the cornice. Fit it around the box, clipping away the excess at corners, and where the batting overlaps, to obtain an even thickness. Dilute white glue to a consistency which spreads easily without leaving ridges or bumps. Glue the batting to the outside and the edges of the cornice, and allow to dry.

Then make a muslin cover to even out the batting before the decorative fabric is applied. Cut the muslin to the dimensions of the batting. Staple it around the back edges, making neat folds at the corners. Pull it evenly taut over the batting so there are no lumps, and staple just inside the face and legs. Trim the excess batting and muslin close to the staples.

Cover with the finish fabric in the same way as for the muslin, trimming away excess at corners so there is no bulkiness.

If the inside of the cornice will be visible at all, you might want to cover the row of staples by gluing a strip of decorative braid over them.

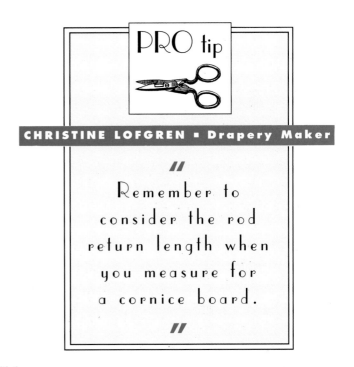

PRO tip

CHRISTINE LOFGREN ■ Drapery Maker

"
Remember to consider the rod return length when you measure for a cornice board.
"

▪ Removable Cornice Cover

A fitted cover can be attached to the cornice with hook and loop tape so that it can be taken down for washing or dry cleaning.

You will need outer fabric and lining, hook and loop tape, and lightweight fusible interfacing.

Cut separate pieces for the face and legs of the cornice from decorator fabric and lining. To the cornice measurements, add 1/2" seam allowance at each side and at the lower edge. Add 1" at the top.

Stitch the side seams in the face fabric, leaving 1" unstitched at the top, Stitch lining seams the same way. Fuse interfacing to the wrong side of the lining. With right sides together, sew the lining to the face fabric around the ends and lower edge, keeping the top open. Turn and press.

Miter the top corners. Clip all seam allowances to the stitching at the top of each seam. Fit over the cornice, matching upper ends of the seams to the corners of the cornice. Fold seam allowances under at the top so the folds meet to form mitered corners. Press. With lining and outer fabric edges together, overcast the raw edges.

Glue or staple the hook strip of the hook and loop tape around the top of the cornice, close to the edge. Sew the loop strip to the underside of the fabric cover in the corresponding position.

▪ Lambrequins ▪

A lambrequin is simply a cornice grown long, extending to the floor at the sides of the window. A lambrequin, like a cornice, can be painted, papered, or covered with fabric. This treatment can serve to emphasize an insignificant window, or it can make a single unit of two or three windows in a row.

To make a lambrequin, allow ease for other elements of the window treatment as described in the instructions for cornices, above. Give careful consideration to proportions when you plan—this window treatment is not subtle!

The lambrequin makes a distinctive window treatment.

▪ Valances ▪

The valance is a very accommodating top treatment. It can be made in virtually any style to coordinate with the curtains or shade below. It is easy to remove for laundering or dry cleaning.

It can also stand on its own when a window covering is not wanted or needed.

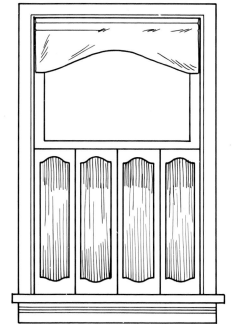

Use matching fabric in the valance and shutter inserts for an easy, yet personalized, treatment.

115

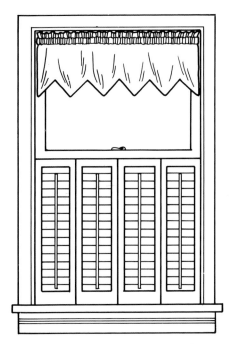

A length of purchased lace makes a delicate top treatment to offset the straight lines of the louvered shutters.

▪ R o d   P o c k e t   V a l a n c e

A valance can be placed on the outer rod of a double rod, or on a rod which is mounted separately. In the latter case, housing space must be allowed for the curtains below (see measuring for cornices, page 113).

A simple, effective valance can be made following the instructions for rod pocket curtains (see page 62). With a casing to fit one—or even two—of the extra-wide valance rods, this is a striking top treatment that works well in many situations.

When a valance is used above curtains or draperies, it can be made to duplicate their style in miniature. It is important, in this case, that the length of the valance be in proportion to the length of the curtains. Hems of the valance should be in proportion to its length.

When a valance constitutes the whole window treatment, it can be made as a shorter version of nearly any style. The hems and headings should be shortened proportionately.

▪ C l o u d   V a l a n c e

Designed to be used alone or above half curtains, this valance is made of sheer or very lightweight fabric that won't restrict light flow, but will soften the lines of the window.

Follow the instructions for the Austrian shade, page 128, but with some changes:

1. Cut fabric twice the width of the window.

2. Adjust the length according to the length measurement for your valance.

3. Use double-cord shirring tape instead of ring tape.

4. At the top, make a rod pocket, with or without heading, according to the instructions on page 62.

5. For the top, use a standard curtain rod with a short return length. Use a small sash rod at the bottom, and mount it at the sides of the window frame if desired.

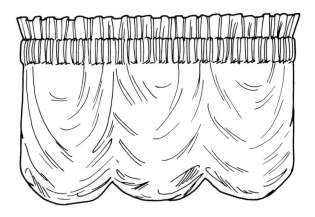

This cloud valance is a shorter, stationary variation of an Austrian shade.

▪ P o u f   V a l a n c e

This soft and pretty topper provides a nice contrast above cafe curtains or half shutters. It's easier to make than it looks! It is simply a rod pocket curtain with a second rod through a casing at the bottom. The lower rod is positioned to allow the fabric to pouf.

You will need two plain curtain rods with about 1" projection, and fabric according to your measurements. A light fabric with some crisp-

116

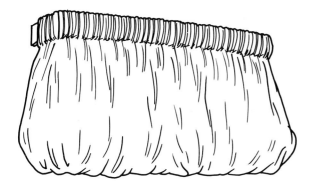

A pouf valance is kept in place by a hidden lower rod.

ness will help this valance hold its shape. Lining can add body if your chosen fabric is too soft.

It is easiest to measure for length if the rods are mounted first. Position the lower rod several inches *above* the point where you want the valance to end. To measure for the finished length, hold the end of a tape measure at the top rod, and hold it against the lower rod, allowing it to loop an inch or two below the lower rod. The bend of the tape will represent the

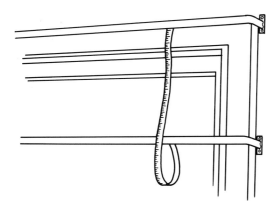

Hold the tape slack to allow for drape of fabric.

finished length of the valance. The point where the tape meets the lower rod will be the finished length measurement you will use to figure the cut length.

Follow the instructions for the rod pocket curtains on page 62. Add a heading at the top, if you wish.

Follow the instructions for the rod pocket curtains on page 62.

The elegant swag, draped casually across the top of a window, is in reality the result of careful planning and construction. The secret lies in cutting the fabric on the bias to give it a smooth, flowing line.

A swag may be draped over a rod, or it can be stapled or tacked to a mounting board. The board or rod should be installed before you measure for the swag. Be sure to allow for clearance around the drapery or curtains below (see measuring for a cornice, page 113). Because the fabric is cut on the bias, certain patterns will not suit this design.

(see measuring for a cornice, page 113)

You will need several yards of muslin to make a pattern. Take rough measurements first. Figure the width of the rod the swag is to cover, and allow the tape measure to drape as you want the top of the swag to do. If you are using a multiple swag, allow for overlap.

Bias-cut fabric produces smooth pleats in a swag.

Working on the bias of the muslin, draw a line to represent the top of the swag, making it the length of your measurement. Mark the center, and draw a line perpendicular to the top and about 3 feet long. At the bottom of that line, draw a line parallel with the top line to indicate the bottom of the swag. The bottom line should be considerably longer than the top line.

Now pin the muslin to the board, or to your work table, positioning the upper corners according to your measurement. At the ends, fold about 6 pleats, folds upward. Pin them in place as you go. Adjust them so the drape at the center reaches the length you determined. When the drape and pleating of the muslin please you, use a waterproof marking pen to draw a line straight across the fabric along the upper front edge of the board or along the top of the rod.

Unfold the muslin, and mark the end points at the bottom line and at the top line. Draw diagonal lines between these points to indicate the sides. Mark the folding points for the pleats along each side. Draw

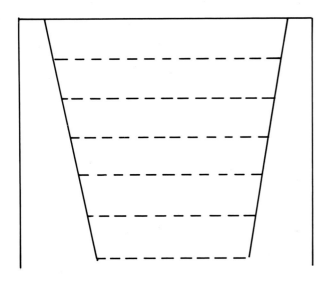

Make up the swag first in muslin to determine accurate draping and pleating.

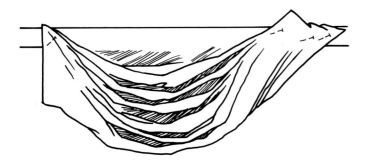

Adjust the pleats with the muslin pinned in place, then cut across the folded fabric.

straight lines across the fabric to join the pleat marks. You will have to adjust here and there so that these lines are parallel.

Now re-pleat the fabric and baste the pleats across the ends. Don't cut anything yet. Try the swag in position again, and adjust the pleats as necessary. Use a different pen color this time. With the pleats still basted, cut carefully across them at the ends. Press your pattern, taking care to press with the grain of the fabric.

If you are using patterned fabric, allow for placement of the design motifs. Place the swag pattern on the bias grain of the fabric. Add 1/2" seam allowance at the lower edge and 1" at the top and sides. Lining also must be cut on the bias. Mark fold points for the pleats on the right side of the lining with a water-soluble fabric pen.

With right sides together, sew the fabric and lining across the lower edge. Turn; press the seam. Stitch the top edges together. Stitch the ends together. Baste the pleats, and try the swag once again. Stitch across the pleats on the ends. Finish the seams with an overcast stitch.

If you want the swag to be removable for cleaning, attach with hook and loop tape, as described for cornices on page 115. Otherwise staple it in place.

▪ Shirred Swag

This top treatment has the graceful drape of the swag above, but is constructed in a completely different way. Because the fabric is cut on the cross grain for this swag, it is a good choice for a patterned fabric that would not look right cut on the bias. It covers just the front of the draperies, not the return portion, so is used with jabots or stationary panels at the ends.

As you can see in the color photographs, pattern placement is important in this swag. Experiment to see where design motifs look best. The photographs can guide you, too, in determining the best length for your swag and number of shirring strips it should have.

The shirred swag is affixed to a mounting board above the curtains or draperies. Read the instructions for the cornice, page 113, to determine size and position for the board. The swag can be stapled or tacked to the board, or can be attached with hook and loop tape as for the cornice cover on page 115.

You will need double shirring tape, one length for each row of shirring and one length for each end. Each length should be about 6" longer than the planned finished length of the swag.

If you will have to piece the fabric for the best pattern positioning or to obtain the necessary width, plan so that seams will be placed at the shirring. When you measure, add 1" for each vertical seam.

Finished width is the same as the width of the mounting board; add 1" for seam allowances. For length, cut the fabric 1-1/2 to 2 times the desired finished length plus 1-1/2" for seam allowances. Cut lining the same size as the face fabric.

1. Stitch vertical seams, if necessary.

2. With right sides together, stitch the face fabric and lining together along the ends and across the lower edge. Turn and press. On the right side, align the upper edges and stitch them together with a serger or overcast stitch.

3. Determine the number of shirring rows the swag will have, and mark their placement. One strip of shirring tape should be placed 1/8" inside each outer edge, and the others spaced evenly across the fabric width.

4. Center each strip at its marked position so several inches of tape extend at top and bottom. Loosen the cords from the tape beyond the edges of the fabric so that the edges of the tape can be trimmed and turned under. Stitch the tapes in position, stitching close to the edges and across both ends, keeping the cords free.

5. Securely knot the cord pairs together at the top of the swag. Draw up the cords from the bottom until the swag measures the desired length. Knot the

cords loosely so adjustments can be made, if necessary, after the swag is mounted.

Jabots

Jabots, or tails, are often used with a swag to balance the drape of the swag. A different color or pattern can be used for the visible lining to tie the decorating scheme together, or just to emphasize the jabots themselves.

Make a muslin pattern so you can make adjustments before you cut into the decorator fabric, and so that you can be sure the jabots are in proportion with the other window treatment elements. Measure the width the finished jabot will occupy. Measure the length the outer edge should be, and that of the inner edge. Measure the rod return, or the projection of the mounting board.

On the muslin, draw a straight line to represent the top, making it approximately double the length of your finished width measurement. At one end, draw a line perpendicular to the top to represent the outer length. At the other end, draw a shorter line to represent length at the inner edge. The inner length might correspond to the length of the swag, or try making it slightly less than half the outer length. At the bottom

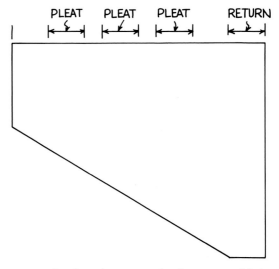

Make the jabot in muslin first to establish the most attractive pleat depth.

of the outer edge, draw a line straight across, the length of the return. Connect this point with

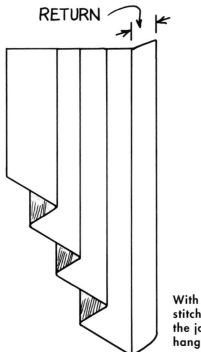

RETURN

With pleats stitched in place, the jabot should hang smoothly.

the lower end of the inner edge. Cut the muslin along the lines.

Now, for trial purposes, measure from the outside edge to a point about 3" beyond the return measurement; mark this point at the top line on the fabric. Pleat the fabric, with the folds toward the outside edge and the first fold at the marked point. Make about three pleats of equal depth, adjusting to obtain your finished width measurement.

Once you are satisfied with the length, proportions, and pleating, mark the muslin accordingly and use it for your pattern. Add 1/2" seam allowances to all sides, then cut the face fabric and lining. If you are making two, be sure to cut a left and a right.

With right sides together, stitch lining to face fabric at sides and lower edge, leaving the top open. Turn and press, then stitch the top closed. Fold pleats; stitch in place across upper edge. Staple or tack them to the rod or top of the mounting board.

PRO tip

KATHRYN LONG ▪ Interior Designer

"

When planning a top treatment, consider the perspective. Have someone else hold up the fabric and rod, and look at it from across the room to see that moldings, rods, and trim will be covered. Also look at the length— it should be in proportion to the length of the panels.

"

▪ Scarves ▪

Here is the window treatment to do before Mom arrives tomorrow! Almost any pretty piece of fabric can become a distinctive window topping in minutes. The fabulous piece of silk you bought in Thailand, the lovely old dresser scarf with Great-grandmother's cutwork, purchased

The fabric's striped pattern inspires the design of a shirred valance and jabots to create a focal point of the small window nook. Holdbacks prevent sheers being buffeted by breezes when the windows are open. Design: Kathryn Long

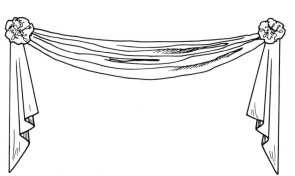

A simple scarf treatment requires no sewing.

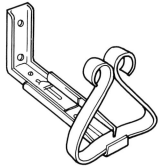

Behind the scene are scarf holders, which allow elaborate draping and knotting to be accomplished in minutes.

scarves and linens—all can work wonders.

There are all kinds of decorative brackets, rods, and holders that can be mounted above or at the ends of the window frame. Hardware stores and flea markets are good sources for out-of-the-ordinary

bits and pieces that can substitute for traditional brackets.

Tulip brackets, made just for this purpose, are available from drapery supply stores. They support the cloth and allow for artistic bows or knots at the ends.

Above: Three pretty scarves, trimmed with Battenberg lace, adorn the window and complement the room's style. Design: Diane Weaver

Right: The casual effect of the draped swag is actually the result of careful arrangement. Lining helps the piece retain its shape, and ends are cut on the bias to hang softly. Design: Ginger Kinzel

SHADES

A new shade can make a major change in the personality of the room with just a minor investment in fabric. Tailored, like Roman shades, or elaborate, like the Austrians, there is a shade style to go with every personal style.

Horizontal tucks on the right side of this Roman shade conceal stitching points of the rings behind. The contrasting lower border meets the valance when the shade is raised to produce an entirely different effect (shown on the next page). Design: Dianne Ingle

· Roman Shades ·

Sleek and compact, Roman shades can adapt to any decor. Their fabric requirements are small, and they don't take long to make. Different fabrics can completely change the character of these shades. Made in a solid color of heavy linen, they are tailored and contemporary. In a sheer fabric, delicate and airy. Roman shades are effective for light control and, when fitted close to the window, are very good insulators. Their simple style makes them perfect companions for interesting top treatments.

Almost any fabric will work for this shade; fabrics with body will pleat better when the shade is opened. In addition to fabric and lining fabric, you will need:

Mounting board, a piece of 1 x 2, the length of the finished shade. If it is mounted outside the window frame the ends will show. You may want to paint it, or cover the ends with fabric. Before you measure for the shade, decide whether the mounting board will be inside or outside the window frame, and whether the 2" side or the 1" side will serve as the face side.

Screw eyes. They attach to the mounting board to carry the cords, so must be large enough that the necessary number of cords will slide easily through them. One is placed above each row of rings. With a very wide shade, or one made of very heavy fabric, **small pulleys** should be used in place of screw eyes.

A small **awning cleat** can be attached to the edge of the window frame to hold the cords neatly.

Ring tape or **individual rings**. Ring tape, with rings attached, eliminates the need for sewing individual rings to the curtain. The vertical ring spacing cannot be altered, however, and the rows of stitching are visible on the right side. Diagram the ring layout (see Step 2, below) before buying tape or rings. Allow enough extra tape for horizontal alignment of the rings.

Shade cord. There is one cord for each vertical row of rings. Each cord must extend from bottom to top of the curtain, across the top, and part way down the side. Allow for knotting, too.

A **weight rod**, brass or galvanized iron, keeps the shade in place. It should be 1/2" shorter than the finished curtain width.

▪ Measuring and Cutting Fabric

Before you begin, read about fabric preparation on page 52. For the finished length of the curtain, measure from the upper front edge of the mounting board, down the front to the desired finish point. For the cut length, add 5" for lower facing, and enough at the top to extend to the back of the mounting board

The finished width can be the inside dimension of the window, or the outside width of the frame. Add 4" for the side hems.

Allow extra for matching patterns (see page 46). If it is necessary to join widths, plan for the seam to be placed over a row of rings.

Lining should be cut to the finished length plus 1", and to the finished width.

124

Pretty and functional, these simple Roman shades are lined to better insulate their windows. Design: Kathryn Long

■ Making the Shade

1. Decide whether to use individual rings or ring tape. Individual rings can be spaced closer, vertically, to produce smaller folds when the shade is open. But sewing them onto the curtain takes more time than does tape. Rings are usually spaced 5" apart on the tape.

2. Draw a diagram of the finished shade and determine ring placement. There should be a vertical row centered over each side hem, tape edges 1/2" from curtain edges. Remaining rows should be spaced 8 to 12" apart. The rings, whether on tape or sewed singly, are spaced in straight horizontal rows.

The bottom horizontal row is 3-1/2" above the bottom of the finished shade. The uppermost rings should be at least 3" from the finished top measurement.

3. Place the face fabric wrong side up on a flat surface. Center the lining over it with top edges even. Fold and press doubled 1" side hems in the face fabric, covering the raw edges of the lining.

Draw a line across the curtain on the lining to represent the finished lower edge.

4. To form the facing, fold the lower edge 5" toward the wrong side; press. Fold a 2" hem along the raw edge of the facing; press. Mark a line across the curtain along the top of the facing. Open out the facing.

5. If you are using ring tape, slipstitch the side hems from the facing line to the edge of the facing. If you are not using ring tape, stitch the entire length of the side hems.

6. Position the ring tape or rings according to your diagram. The bottom row should be about 1/2" above the facing line, but the tape should extend below the facing line. Cut rings off if necessary. At the top, allow tape to extend to the top of the curtain, but cut off rings above those designated as the top row (Step 2).

7. Stitch tape in place; a zipper foot may work best for this. Or sew on individual rings: fold fabric wrong side out on the horizontal line indicating a row of rings. You may be able to sew them by machine with a button foot, or with a zigzag stitch and the feed dogs lowered. Knot threads securely.

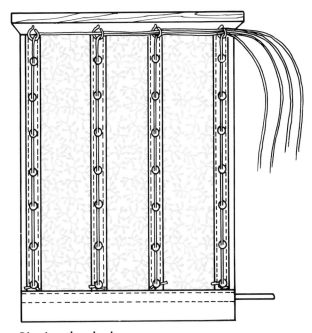

Rigging the shade

8. Fold facing up to the marked line. Stitch it in place across the curtain, close to the fold. Stitch again 1-1/2" from the previous stitching to form the rod casing. On the sides, hand-stitch facing to curtain from lower edge to casing.

9. Overcast the upper edge, catching tape ends in the stitching.

▪ Rigging and Mounting the Shade

1. Align the finish line on the shade with upper front edge of the mounting board. Staple or tack the shade securely to the top of the board.

2. Attach a screw eye or pulley to the underside of the board above each vertical line of rings.

3. With the shade wrong side up on a table, thread the cords through the rings. First decide whether the shade will draw from the left or from the right, (remember it's wrong side up!) and begin at the opposite side. Tie an end of a cord securely to the bottom ring, thread it up through the rings in its row, and

through the rings on the mounting board to the opposite side of the shade. Leave it long enough to almost reach the bottom of the shade. Repeat with another cord through the next vertical row, and so on.

4. Mount the shade. Put the rod into its casing.

5. With the shade lowered, adjust the cords so the tension is equal. Knot them together just outside the screw eye on the draw side. Then braid them together to the desired length, and knot the ends. Affix the cleat to the edge of the window frame.

The balloon shade's fullness provides a soft accent for a little girl's room. This shade is made with a casing at the top so it can be used with a curtain rod rather than being mounted on a board. Design: Pam Long

Thick corded piping at the top and a ruffle at the lower edge of the shirred balloon shade repeat colors of the room's wallpaper border and painted trim. Design: Donna Evans

Pleated Balloon Shade

A Roman shade with box pleats added to give it fullness, the balloon shade has a softer, less tailored appearance. To give it better draping quality, this one is unlined.

The materials needed are the same as for the Roman shade, page 124, except that individual rings are used here instead of ring tape. The fabric should be soft rather than crisp, light to medium weight. If it is necessary to piece the width of the panel, plan the pleats first so that the seam can be placed inside a pleat.

Determine the finished length and width for the shade. Add 12" for the cut length. Cut width should be 2 to 2-1/2 times the finished width measurement, depending upon the weight of the fabric. Cut a strip for the facing 3" long, and as wide as the finished width measurement plus 1".

Before you begin, read about fabric preparation, page 52, and about basic sewing techniques, page 54.

This box-pleated balloon shade is affixed to a mounting board set into the window frame.

1. Stitch 1" doubled hems along the sides of the shade.

2. To figure pleats, measure the hemmed width of the shade, and cut a paper strip that length. There should be a half pleat at each side, folded toward the edge of the shade. Space the others evenly across, allowing 8 to 12" between them.

3. Using the paper template as a guide, pleat the fabric and press the pleats in place the full length of the shade.

4. At the top, stitch across the pleats close to the edge, and again at the point which marks the finished length of the shade.

5. Stitch across the pleats at the bottom of the shade, about 3/8" from the edge.

6. Press to the wrong side 1/2" at each short end of the facing strip. Fold it in half lengthwise, wrong sides together. Pin it to the lower edge of the shade, on the right side, aligning the raw edges. Stitch, and over cast the raw edges. Press to the wrong side.

7. Mark positions for the rings. There should be a vertical row at each side hemline and centered between each pair of pleats. The bottom horizontal row of rings is on the facing fold; space remaining horizontal rows about 5" apart. The top row should be at least 3" below the finish point at the top. Stitch

the rings, taking care to stitch through only one fabric layer. See Step 7, page 125.

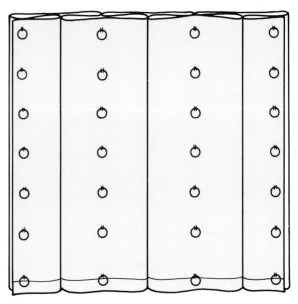

Vertical rows of rings are sewed behind the pleats and will not be seen from the front of the shade.

8. In each vertical row, tie the bottom three rings together. Then rig and mount the shade according to the instructions on page 126. Slip the weight rod into its casing at the bottom of the shade.

■ A u s t r i a n   S h a d e ■

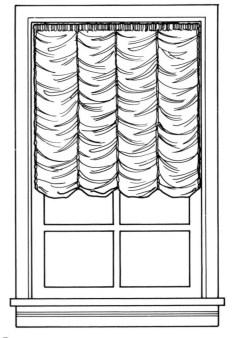

The Austrian shade is similar to a Roman shade with fullness added by shirring between the vertical rows of rings.

Versatile in its design, the balloon shade adapts well to informal or sophisticated decorating schemes. Here its happy mix of patterns is continued with the cushions below. Design: Donna Williams

An elegant cousin of the Roman shade, the Austrian shade has vertical shirring between the cords. Soft fabric which drapes well is the best choice for this shade. Lining fabric should have the same draping quality as the face fabric; a lightweight cotton or cotton/polyester blend would perform better than standard lining fabric. In addition to the fabrics, you will need:

Mounting board, a piece of 1 x 2, the length of the finished shade. If it is mounted outside the window frame the ends will show, and should be painted or covered with fabric. Before you measure for the shade, decide whether the mounting board will be inside or outside the window frame. Because the shape of this shade is not well defined, it may be better to mount it outside the frame. Decide, too, whether the 2" side or the 1" side will serve as the face side.

Screw eyes. They attach to the mounting board to carry the cords, so must be large enough that the necessary number of cords will slide easily through them. One is placed above each row of rings. With a very wide shade, or one made of very heavy fabric, **small pulleys** should be used in place of screw eyes.

A small **awning cleat** can be attached to the edge of the window frame to hold the cords neatly.

Special **Austrian shade tape** has a double row of cords for shirring, as well as rings to carry the draw cords. You will need one length of tape for each scalloped row, plus one extra. Each length should be the cut length of the shade plus about 4". Allow extra for horizontal alignment of the rings.

Shade cord. There is one cord for each vertical row of rings. Each cord must extend from bottom to top of the curtain, across the top, and part way down the side. Allow for knotting, too.

A **weight rod**, wood or metal, keeps the shade in place at the bottom. It should be 1" shorter than the finished curtain width.

▪ Measuring and Cutting Fabric

Finished length is measured from the upper front edge of the mounting board. At the lower edge it is somewhat variable because of the drape of the scallops. Measure to the point where the cords between scallops should end. Cutting length depends on the weight of the fabric. For sheers, use 3 times the finished length. For light to medium fabrics, use 2-1/2 times the finished length. Add at the top the distance from the finished top to the back of the mounting board. Add 1" for the bottom hem.

To figure width, you first have to decide how many rows of scallops the shade will have. A scallop can be as narrow as 8" across in sheer fabric, or as wide as 14" for medium-weight fabric. An average is 10 to 12". Figure space for scallops at 2" less than the finished width measurement. Determine, too, how much drape you want in each scallop row. Add 2" per scallop for slight drape; 4" for considerable drape.

If the fabric must be pieced to obtain the necessary width, plan so the seam will be at the tape placement point. If you are working with a pattern which requires matching, see pages 57 and 58 for specific information.

Lining fabric should be cut to the same length as the face fabric, and 3" narrower. Plan the position of any necessary vertical seams as for the face fabric.

▪ Making the Shade

Before you begin, read about fabric preparation, page 52, and about sewing techniques, page 54.

1. Join widths in face fabric and lining, if necessary.

2. Turn 1-1/2" to the wrong side along each side; press.

3. Place the lining on the wrong side of the shade; align top and bottom edges and tuck side edges under the hems.

4. Place a length of tape along each side, 1"

inside the edge. Position it so that a ring is placed 2" above the lower edge. Position the remaining lengths of tape, making sure that the rings are aligned horizontally, and pin them in place.

5. Stitch along both sides of each tape, ending the stitching at the bottom ring on the tape. A zipper foot may work best for this.

6. At the top, free the ends of the cords. Knot each pair together securely.

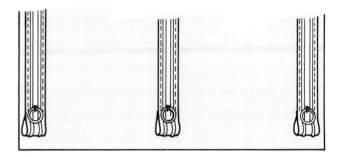

Stitch cord ends below the bottom rings.

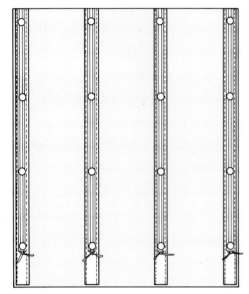

Tapes are left loose at the bottom, then turned up and stitched to form carriers for the rod.

7. Zigzag the face fabric and lining together along the top, keeping the cords free but catching the tape ends in the stitching.

8. At the bottom of the shade, free the cords to just below the bottom rings. Tie each pair together with a secure square knot.

9. To form a carrier for the rod, fold the lower, unstitched end of each tape up to the first ring. Fold the raw edge under and stitch by hand to the tape, just under the ring. Stitch through the tape only, not through the outer fabric.

10. Fold the lower edge 1" to the wrong side, press, and fold the raw edge in to the crease. Press again, and stitch.

11. Place the shade on a padded work table,

wrong side up. Straighten the lower edge. Pin it securely to the table. From the top, draw up the cords, one pair at a time, until the shade measures the finished length plus molding allowance.

12. Sew a cover for the rod. Measure the diameter, add 1/2" for ease and 1/2" for seam allowances. For the length, add 1" to the rod length measurement. Cut the piece from a scrap of the face fabric or lining. With right sides together, stitch across one end and along the long edges, 1/4" from the outer edge. Turn right side out with a tube turner, or thread a darning needle with several lengths of thread, take several stitches through the seam allowance at the sewn end, and pull the needle through the tube, pulling the tube right side out. Insert the rod, tuck in the end, and slipstitch across. Slip the rod through the loops on the shade. Stitch the cover to the loops to keep it in place.

13. On the mounting board, mark the positions of the curtain shirring strips. Mark 1" from each end, and space the others evenly across the board. Attach a screw eye or pulley to the bottom of the board at each mark.

14. Tack or staple the top of the' shade to the board, matching marks on the board to shirring strips. Make small pleats to take up excess fabric. Do not tack through the cords.

15. Try the mounted shade at the window, and make any necessary length adjustments. Secure the knots at the top.

16. Thread the cords through the rings on the shade. See Step 3, page 126.

17. Hang the shade at its window. With the shade lowered, adjust the cords so the tension is equal. Knot them together just outside the screw eye on the draw side. Then braid them together to the desired length, and knot the ends. Affix the cleat to the edge of the window frame.

▪ R o l l e r   S h a d e ▪

A simple and efficient window treatment, a roller shade can play an important part in the decorating scheme. A top treatment can be added to enhance the simple lines of the shade: a plain valance, for example. Or it could provide a contrast in line, like a swag.

A shade is best mounted inside the window frame, where it more effectively controls light and increases energy efficiency. Because the shade should fit well, it is especially important to measure accurately. Check measurements at several points along the width and length, and check the corners with a carpenter's square.

Fabric for this shade should be medium to fairly heavy, and quite stable. Glazed fabrics are not a good choice; abrasion will crack and wear the glaze. Heavily finished fabrics and those treated to repel soil or moisture may not bond well to the backing. Test a sample.

Cut the fabric 12" longer than the finished length measurement, and about 2" wider. The sides will be trimmed to the finished width after the fabric is bonded to the backing. You will also need:

Roller to fit the window width.

Fusible shade backing, cut to fabric dimensions.

Wooden slat to support the lower edge, cut 1/2" shorter than the finished width measurement.

Decorative shade pull.

1. Fuse the backing to the wrong side of the fabric, following manufacturer's instructions. Allow to cool, then test the bond. Some dry cleaners provide a fabric-bonding service; their equipment is better for the job than most home irons.

3. Carefully trim the edges to the finished width measurement. A rotary cutter with a sharp blade, or a sharp craft knife, used with a straightedge, is best for this.

4. Lightly rub white glue along the edges to prevent raveling.

5. Fold a 1-1/2" single hem at the lower edge. Stitch across, 1/4" from the raw edge, to form a slat casing.

6. Determine whether the shade will roll over or under the roller. With the pin on the end of the roller at the right, it will roll under.

7. Staple the shade to the roller, taking care to keep it straight. Attach the pull at the center near the lower edge, through the fabric and into the slat.

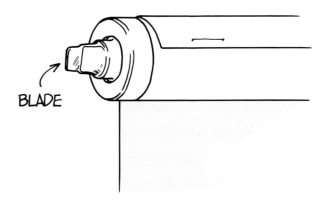

BLADE

For a conventional roll, where the shade rolls onto the roller from underneath, attach the shade to the roller with the pin end of the roller to the right and the blade end to the left. For a reverse roll—the shade goes over the roller—attach the shade to the roller with the blade end of the roller to the right. With the conventional roll the shade will lie close against the window.

A harmonious blend of patterns enhances the elegant design of this den window covering. The face of the padded cornice is curved and trimmed with piping. Stationary side panels hang outside the cornice to frame the Roman shade behind. Design: Ginger Kinzel

FINISHING
TOUCHES

A small design detail or accessory can turn a plain window treatment into one that is unique and wonderful. Professional designers know how to work magic with trims and embellishments, and the results can be seen in the photographs. Here are instructions for some basic accessories; use your imagination to make them work for you.

Left: Small touches can make a window treatment something special. The poufy knots of fabric, made by looping the material over brackets, add extra pizzazz. Design: Pam Long

Above: Fabric rosettes bring a delicate color accent to the ends of a sheer lace swag. Design: Donna Evans

Above right: A brilliant finish for a superb design, cord in the colors of the fabric print lies along the upper edge of the valance. A knot defines each pleat. Design: Kathryn Long

Right: A rosette made up of both fabrics used in the swags and jabots occupies a place of honor atop this formal window dressing. Design: Pam Long

135

Above: Thick cord defines the gentle curve along the base of the curtain heading. Tiebacks are finer cord in the same color. Design: Donna Evans

Above right: Curtain tiebacks repeat in miniature the design of the valance shown on page 66. Piping and a narrow box-pleated ruffle are sewn into the seam along the lower edge. Design: Ginger Kinzel

Lower right: Carefully constructed bows trimmed to match the lining of the valance add flair. Design: Drew Atkinson

Cords

Beautiful, silky cording, available from drapery supply stores, is an elegant embellishment. It adds a texture and it can tie a color scheme together. It is perfect for tiebacks. It can be draped along a decorative rod to create a simple top treatment.

Under the heading of pleated draperies, a length of cord creates a horizontal line of interest. The cord can be draped slightly between pleats, then knotted at the base of each pleat. It is then stitched to the heading by hand.

Cording is available with an attached welting, allowing it to be sewn into the seam on a tieback, or stapled at the edge of a fabric-covered cornice. Welted cording adds interest to plain draperies when sewed into a facing seam along the leading edges.

Tiebacks

With many curtains tiebacks are a practical necessity, and there is no reason they can't be decorative as well. The placement of the tiebacks affects the overall look of the curtains; their position should relate to some horizontal element—the window sill, the midpoint of the window sash, the top of sheer half curtains behind, even a muntin strip. Tiebacks seem to look best at a slant, with the low, inner curve corresponding with the horizontal reference point.

Shaped Tieback

To make a tieback that fits well, cut a doubled strip of kraft paper to the width you prefer and pin it, cut edges downward, around the curtain. Adjust it to find the best slant and length for the tieback. Draw a vertical line across the ends that will indicate the angle. Mark the center point of the tieback end on the edge of the window frame, or on the wall if the outer edges of the curtains extend past the frame.

Unfold the paper to use as a pattern. Cut two tiebacks, a left and a right, adding 1/2" seam

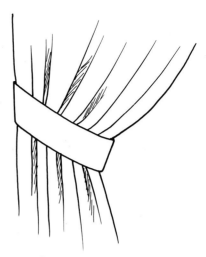

Determine the angle of the tieback ends by measuring with a paper template.

allowance on all sides. Cut two strips of fusible interfacing to the size of the folded pattern, without adding seam allowance.

Crease the tieback at the fold line as with the paper. Open it out and fuse interfacing to the wrong side, following the manufacturer's instructions. The interfaced side will be the *inside* of the tieback as it goes around the curtain.

Fold under the seam allowances at the ends; press. With right sides together, stitch the long ends. Turn, and press.

Stitch across the ends.

Tack a ring to each end. Attach a cup hook or decorative tieback holder to the outer edge of the window frame or wall at the marked point.

There are many ways to vary this tieback. A bias strip could be used to bind the edges and to add a second color. A piece of purchased trim or ribbon might be centered along the outside.

A decorative machine embroidery stitch could be used to topstitch the edges.

Piped Tieback

Corded piping, either purchased or made to match, makes a custom accessory of a utilitarian tieback. Piping can be a solid color chosen to coordinate with a print, or vice versa. Piping can add a new element with a contrasting color, pattern, or texture.

Measure for this tieback as for the Shaped Tieback, above. but use a single thickness of kraft paper. For each tieback, you will need purchased piping, or cording to make the piping, twice the length of your finished measurement, plus 4". You will also need a small amount of lightweight fusible interfacing, and two small rings.

From doubled fabric, position the paper pattern, add 1/2" seam allowance to all edges, and cut. From the pattern, cut two pieces of fusible interfacing without seam allowances. Fuse a piece of interfacing to the wrong side of each fabric piece.

Position piping along the long edges of the tieback piece, on the right side, with piping raw edges toward the tieback raw edges. Curve the ends so that the cord crosses into the tieback seam allowance 1/2" from each end. Align piping stitching line with the tieback seamline. Stitch.

With right sides together and the piping sandwiched between, place the piped tieback section on the other tieback section, aligning raw edges. Stitch along both long edges, on the previous stitching line. Turn, and press.

Trim excess piping at the ends. Turn end seam allowances to the inside; press. Stitch by hand, or stitch close to the edge by machine. Sew on rings.

▪ P i p i n g

Easy to make, piping lends a professional finish to the edges of a covered cornice, to a valance, or to tiebacks. Piping looks best if fabric strips are cut on the bias, especially if the fabric is very stable.

Purchase cording in a diameter that will be appropriate for the purpose. Thick cording would make piping suitable for the edges of a cornice over a large window; finer cord would be suitable to trim tiebacks.

Measure the diameter of the cord and add 1". Cut bias strips to this width and slightly longer than the piping length needed.

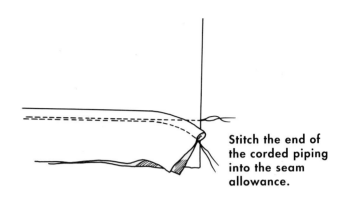

Stitch the end of the corded piping into the seam allowance.

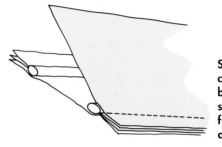

Sandwich the corded piping between right sides of the fabric, aligning all raw edges.

These strips are easiest to cut using a rotary cutter and straightedge. If you need to piece fabric strips to make up the necessary length, seam them on the grain of the fabric, as shown in the illustration.

Fold a fabric strip, right side out, over the cord. With the zipper foot or cording foot, stitch the fabric close to the cord.

If the piping will be used on a curved edge, clip the seam allowance almost to the stitching at 1/2" intervals to allow the piping to curve smoothly.

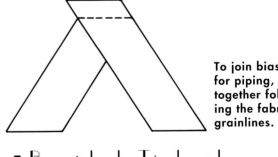

To join bias strips for piping, stitch together following the fabric grainlines.

▪ B r a i d e d   T i e b a c k

This simple accessory makes a big impact. Use the curtain fabric, or use several solid colors to pick up the colors in the print of the curtain, or use something completely different to complement the curtain or coordinate with the top treatment.

For each tieback, you will need thick cording, about eight times the finished length of the tieback. You also will need two small rings, and a tieback holder or cup hook.

Measure for the tieback by holding a tape around the curtain at the correct angle. For each tieback, cut 3 lengths of cording each twice as long as the finished tieback measurement plus 1". Measure the diameter of the cording.

Cut a strip of fabric for each length of cording, 5/8" wider than the cord diameter, and 1" longer than the finished length measurement.

Wrap a strip of fabric around one end of a cord, wrong side out, long raw edges together, so that the fabric and cord are aligned at one end. With the zipper foot on the machine, stitch securely across the aligned ends through the cord and fabric, pivot, and stitch along the long fabric edges with the

Cut cord twice the length of the fabric; begin stitching at the center of the cord length.

presser foot fairly close to the cord, but not tight against it. Be careful not to catch the cord in the stitching. Trim seam allowances to 1/8". Then ease the fabric tube right side out and over the cord. Clip away 1/2" of cord at each end, turn under the fabric ends and stitch them. Repeat for the other strips.

Clamp the ends of three cords to a table, and braid them together. Stitch the ends together. Sew a ring at each end. Repeat for the other tieback.

■ Cord and Tassel Tieback

If you can't find cord in exactly the right color, or if you just want to try the technique, this custom cord will give your curtains a very distinctive look.

Find yarn—a good bit of it—in a color or several colors to coordinate with your curtains. Yarn with some rayon content will produce a cord with some sheen to it; cotton or wool will have a softer, dull finish.

1. Cut yarn to lengths about eight times the desired finished length of the tieback. Use enough strands to make a thick cord; the finished diameter will be approximately double the diameter of the yarn.

2. Knot the lengths at one end, and fasten this securely to a table with a clamp. Or find an assistant to hold it for you. Holding the yarn taut, twist the yarn until it tries to double on itself. Then clamp the working end together with the beginning, keeping the cord taut.

3. Now ease up on the tension and let the cord twist around itself. Even out the cord; knot the ends together.

4. For the tassel, find a stiff piece of cardboard, or other object, about half an inch longer than you want the finished tassel to be. Wrap yarn around the cardboard. The more yarn, the fuller the tassel.

5. Cut through the yarn along one edge of the cardboard. Hold the yarn pieces at the center, and arrange them around the knot of the cord, keeping the centers of the yarn pieces just above the knot on the cord.

6. Tie the bundle securely around its center, above the knotted cord, with a strong thread or

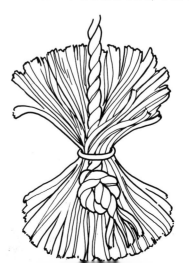

Arrange and tie the yarn pieces above the knot in the cord.

yarn. Pull the upper ends of the yarn down over the lower ones. Arrange them smoothly. Wrap yarn around, tightly, at a point below the knot. Thread the yarn end through a yarn needle and work it into the tassel.

7. Attach a tieback holder or cup hook as described in the Shaped Tieback instructions, above. Slip the tieback up over the curtain.

▪ C h o u x R o s e t t e ▪

A pretty ornament for tieback ends or for finishing the ends of a draped swag, these little "cabbage roses" can be made of your curtain fabric or in a complementary material. The instructions produce a rosette approximately 5" in diameter.

You will need a piece of decorator fabric, 12" square; 2 scraps of medium to heavy cotton fabric,

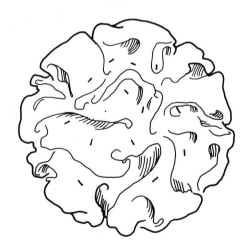

Hand stitching creates the petals of the rosette.

4" square, for the backing; a 4" piece of paper-backed fusible interfacing.

1. Fuse the interfacing to one of the cotton scraps. Draw a circle, 4" in diameter, on the cloth. Peel off the backing and fuse to the other cotton scrap. Cut

around the circle. Draw two intersecting lines on the circle to divide it into quarters.

2. Machine baste around the fabric square, stitching one row 1/2" inch from the edge, the second row 1/8" inside the first, breaking the stitching at each corner and leaving long thread tails.

3. Draw up the threads so that each side of the square fits one quarter of the circle, fitting the edges of the square over the edges of the circle. Secure the ends of the gathering threads. Hand-stitch the edges of the square in place at the back of the circle. The piece should resemble a shower cap now.

4. With needle and thread, tack the fabric into folds and tucks over the surface of the circle to give it the rosette shape and form. The more stitching, the more "petals" the rosette will have. Allow some of the fabric to extend beyond the edges to cover the gathering stitches. Tack the rosette in place.

▪ B i a s R o s e t t e

A perfect finish at the upper corners of a swag or cornice, this soft fabric flower is fun to make. The length and width of the fabric strip will determine the finished size of the rosette. This rosette will be approximately 6" in diameter.

Cut a bias strip of fabric 60" long and 6" wide. If it is necessary to piece the fabric to obtain the length, join the strips as described in the instructions for making piping on page 138.

Fold the strip in half lengthwise, right side out. Do not press the fold. Loosen the machine's upper thread tension by one number. Beginning 1/2" from one end, stitch from the fold across the end, curving the stitching line toward the long raw edges, and continuing to the other end, using 1/2" seam allowance. Curve the stitching across the end to the fold. Working on the same side of the fabric, sew another row of stitching 1/8" away from the first, in the seam allowance. Leave long thread tails.

To gather up the fabric, pull gently on the bobbin threads, working from each end toward the center of

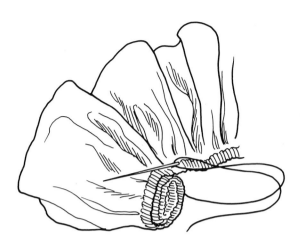

Roll and stitch the gathered bias strip to shape the rosette.

the strip. Draw up the fabric as tightly as possible.

Have ready a threaded hand sewing needle. Starting at one end of the strip, roll the strip tightly for several turns. Stitch in place through the seam allowance, leaving the thread attached. Continue rolling, more loosely as the rosette grows in diameter, stitching in place after every few turns. Tuck in the end and stitch it in place, then arrange the "petals".

▪ C o v e r e d   R o d s ▪

For curtains which are not opened and closed, a thick rod covered with the curtain fabric between the panels can make the difference between just curtains and a window treatment.

For a **smooth covering**, cut fabric 2" longer than the area you wish to cover. Cut the length on the cross grain of the fabric. In width, the piece should be the diameter of the rod plus 1-1/2".

On the rod, draw a straight line for placement. Along one long edge of the fabric, fold 3/4" to the wrong side, press.

Starting at the center and working toward the ends, place the raw edge of the fabric against the line on the rod, wrap, so that the folded edge overlaps. Secure with masking tape. Staple near the fold.

A fabric-covered rod becomes an important element in the overall design.

For a **shirred rod covering**, cut fabric as above, but to the rod diameter add 1/4" ease and 1/2" for seam allowances. Cut the strip twice as long as the rod length to be covered.

With right sides together, stitch the long edges with 1/4" seam allowance. Turn and press. Slip it over the rod, adjusting the gathers. A staple here and there at the back of the rod will keep the fabric in place.

Acknowledgments

Contributing Designers

Drew B. Atkinson
Studio III
25 Alclare Dr.
Asheville, NC 28804

Gail Britt
Britt's Home Interiors
35 Mayflower Dr.
Asheville, NC 28804

Donna Evans
425 Rowland Rd.
Swannanoa, NC 28778

Rosaleen Feeser
Creative Concepts
11 Hickory Drive
Weaverville, NC 28787

Dianne Ingle
Drapery Arts Interiors
709 Hwy. 70
Swannanoa, NC 28778

Ginger Kinzel
About the House Design
1800 Hendersonville Rd.
Asheville, NC 28803

Kathryn Long
Ambience Interiors
27 Broadway
Asheville, NC 28801

Pam Long
Pam Long Interiors
22 Autumn Ridge Ln.
Asheville, NC 28803

Susan Nilsson
1000 Hendersonville Rd.
Asheville, NC 28803

Ruby Haynes
RSVP Interiors
6 Boston Way
Asheville, NC 28803

Diane Weaver
Weaverville, NC 28787

Donna Williams
Leicester, NC 28748

Location Photography

We'd like to thank the homeowners who graciously allowed us to photograph their window treatments.

Drew Atkinson, Dr. Lisa Behnke, Sue Bodvig, Kim Clements, Sally Crum, Debbie Denton, Anna Friedman, Ruby Haynes, Joseph and Karen Herrin, Kathryn Long, Pam Long, Sarah Long, Jerome and Adrienne Oliver, Gail Smith, Jill Stowe, Patricia Trachsel, Diane Weaver, Susan White, Kim Wiggins, Donna Williams, Christine Wood

Additional Photography

J. Weiland, Asheville, North Carolina, photo page 72 bottom.
Photo © J. Weiland

And Thanks To...

The staff of the Kirsch Division of Cooper Industries, Inc., for their assistance with the hardware illustrations.

Peggy Wilkinson, fabric consultant; Merle Ball and Christine Lofgren, drapery makers; and Hazel Witt, interior designer, for their tips on technique.

Metric Conversion Chart

Although the conversions aren't exact, there are about 2-1/2 centimeters in an inch. So to convert inches to centimeters, just multiply the number of inches by 2.5. To convert feet to meters, divide the number of feet by 3.25.

INCHES	MILLIMETERS
1/8	3
1/4	6
1/2	13
3/4	19

INCHES	CENTIMETERS
1	2.5
1-1/4	3.2
1-1/2	3.8
1-3/4	4.4
2	5
3	7.5
4	10
5	12.5
6	15
7	17.5
8	20
9	22.5
10	25
11	27.5
12	30
13	32.5
14	35
15	37.5
16	40
17	42.5
18	45
19	47.5
20	50
21	52.5
22	55
23	57.5
24	60
25	62.5
26	65
27	67.5
28	70
29	72.5
30	75

Index